big mama's
BACK IN THE KITCHEN

Charlene Johnson

A STOKE GABRIEL ENTERPRISES, INCORPORATED PUBLICATION

compiled & edited
    Charlene Johnson

culture & research consultant
    Cottrell Wrenn, Jr.

production consultant
    Wayne Tanner

cover art
    Ronnie Barnes

cover design
    David Crain
    Ken Juneau & Associates

Publisher Stoke Gabriel Enterprises, Incorporated
PO Box 12060   Alexandria, Louisiana 71315
Telephone (318) 487-9577   Fax (318) 487-4667

*O*n the banks of historic Cane River at Melrose Plantation's annual Arts and Crafts Fair, the first copy of *Big Mama's Old Black Pot Recipes* was sold in June, 1987. Since that day customers from all 50 states and numerous foreign countries have responded in over-whelming numbers to *That Old Black Pot*. As orders poured in from across the country, an amazing realization became evident, legions of regional as well as transplanted Southerners were eager to revisit childhood memories rooted in the Depression Era of the Rural South. Notes and letters from the most unlikely locations related special recollections brought back by *Big Mama's*. And the most astonishing aspect of this story is that the orders, letters, and notes are still coming. In response to this tremendous acceptance, a follow-up publication, *Big Mama's Back in the Kitchen*, will serve up another heaping helping of delicious food and Southern hospitality.

*T*hanks, customers! This collection of recipes and memories is dedicated to each of you.

NOTES ABOUT THE BOOK

The recipes are simple, directions easy to follow, and the food tastes as if Big Mama has been in the kitchen.

The variety of foods reflects the unique heritage of blended cultures rooted in the Deep South.

The short stories and vignettes are from real life accounts of fond remembrances from times long past.

The art tells a story and brings back forgotten images.

The cooks, the writers, the designers, the artists, the consultants, and the publisher are Southern born, Southern reared, and Southern proud.

There's nothing like that old black pot.

The original Dutch oven was a three-legged cast-iron pot that could be used in the fireplace over hot coals or outdoors over an open fire. Meats, stews, and soups could be simmered for hours. Breads, cakes, and puddings were baked by placing a small pan or rack inside the large cast-iron pot. A skilled hand outstretched over the fire was the only way to judge the best cooking or baking temperature.

Later, the Dutch oven was modified for wood-burning stoves. Today, cast-iron cookery is used in many of the most modern kitchens in the South as well as throughout the country. Several of the recipes in this publication recommend use of that old black pot.

appetizers and beverages

tiny meat pie appetizers, **12**

fiesta pinwheels, **13**

party meatballs, **14**

party piggies, **15**

miniature crawfish balls, **16**

chili-pepper shrimp / marinated shrimp, **17**

seafood dip / crab dip, **18**

smoked salmon log / salmon spread, **19**

chicken salad spread / deviled eggs, **20**

layered cheese roll, **21**

taco cheese dip, **22**

artichoke dip / guacamole, **23**

hot spinach dip, **24**

spicy vegetable dip / sun-dried tomato dip, **25**

fruit dip / marshmallow fruit dip, **26**

granny's parched peanuts, **27**

spiced pecans / orange flavored walnuts, **28**

cider punch / spiced citrus tea, **29**

slushy party punch / grape lemonade punch, **30**

orange sherbet punch / raspberry sherbet punch, **31**

southern coffee punch, **32**

TINY MEAT PIE APPETIZERS

FILLING

2 pounds ground beef

1 (1.5-ounce) package spaghetti mix

1 teaspoon chili powder

1/2 cup chopped ripe olives

1/4 cup finely chopped jalapeño peppers

PASTRY

2 (8-ounce) packages cream cheese (softened)

2 cups margarine (softened)

1/2 teaspoon salt

5 cups flour

1 egg

FILLING

Brown meat in skillet. Drain excess liquid. Add remaining filling ingredients to meat mixture. Cook over medium heat 5 minutes, stirring constantly. Set meat aside to cool.

PASTRY

Blend cream cheese, margarine, and salt. Add flour, 1 cup at a time. Mix well after each addition. (Dough will be very stiff.) Cover and chill 3-4 hours.

Beat egg until creamy. Set aside.

When ready to make pies, sprinkle a thin layer of flour over a large piece of wax paper. Divide dough into 3 equal portions. Roll layer of dough into a thin circular shape. (Dough is easier to handle if rolled out between 2 pieces of floured wax paper.) Roll out to approximately 1/8-inch thickness. Use a 3-inch cutter to make circles. Spoon 1 teaspoon meat mixture onto center of circle. Fold pastry over and pinch edges together. Flatten edges to totally seal mixture inside. Use fork tines to flatten edges. Lightly brush tops and edges of pies with egg mixture. Pierce top once with fork. Place on ungreased cookie sheet.

Bake at 400 degrees - 10-12 minutes or until lightly browned around edges.

To freeze pies before baking, lay on baking sheet until frozen. Store in plastic bags.

FIESTA PINWHEELS

2 (8-ounce) packages
cream cheese
(softened)

1 (1.1-ounce) package
Hidden Valley Fiesta
Dip Mix

1 (4-ounce) jar
chopped pimiento
(drained)

1 (2-1/2-ounce) can
black olives (finely
chopped)

5 whole green onions
(finely chopped)

1/2 cup finely chopped
bell pepper

1 (8-inch) package
flour tortillas

Blend cream cheese and Fiesta Dip Mix until thoroughly mixed. Add chopped vegetables. Mix until filling is smooth. Refrigerate overnight to enhance flavor.

Spread a thin layer evenly over tortillas leaving extreme outer edges without spread. Roll into a tight pinwheel. Chill thoroughly. Use an electric knife to cut into thin slices.

Add sour cream (1-2 Tablespoons) if mixture is too stiff. Green olives and celery may be substituted for black olives and bell pepper.

Junior has lived all his life in southern river towns from the Mississippi Delta near Memphis to the Red in Louisiana. He shares a fond memory about his grandmother. "At least once a month, on Sunday afternoon, Daddy, Mamadea, and the five 'kids' walked four miles to Mama Beck's house. When we arrived, the table was set for an early supper. She always served a spicy goulash, buttermilk biscuits with butter, ice cold lemonade, and a surprise dessert. Everyone would have a place around the old wooden table. We ate heartily and visited together. As we were leaving, Mama Beck always said, 'the company has been good, ya'll come back real soon'."

PARTY MEATBALLS

MEATBALLS

1 pound ground beef
1 cup seasoned bread
   crumbs
2 Tablespoons finely
   chopped onions
1 Tablespoon finely
   chopped green onions
1 clove garlic (minced)
2 Tablespoons barbecue
   sauce
1 teaspoon horseradish
2 eggs (slightly beaten)
3/4 teaspoon Creole
   seasoning
2 Tablespoons grated
   Parmesan cheese
1/3 cup olive oil

Combine all ingredients, except olive oil. Mix thoroughly. Form into 1-inch meatballs. Brown meatballs in hot oil. Drain excess liquid.

SPICY DIPPING SAUCE

1/2 cup catsup
1/2 cup brown sugar
1/4 cup cider vinegar
1 Tablespoon Worcester-
   shire sauce
2 teaspoons hot sauce
1 teaspoon salt
1 teaspoon accent
1/2 teaspoon dry mustard
1/4 teaspoon pepper
1/4 teaspoon liquid smoke
2 Tablespoons finely
   chopped onion

Combine all ingredients in a small saucepan. Bring mixture to a boil. Reduce heat and simmer 15 minutes.

PARTY PIGGIES

2 cups apple jelly
1 cup barbecue sauce
1/3 cup mustard
1 (3-pound) package
    smoked cocktail
    sausage

Combine apple jelly, barbecue sauce, and mustard in a large saucepan. Bring mixture to a rolling boil. Add sausage. Simmer over low heat 1 hour.

Make alternate sauce by combining 1 [12-ounce] bottle chili sauce, 1 [10-ounce] jar grape jelly, and 1/4 cup white wine.

MINIATURE CRAWFISH BALLS

1 pound crawfish tails
1/4 cup finely chopped
parsley
1/4 cup finely chopped
green onion tops
1/4 cup finely chopped
bell pepper
1-1/4 teaspoons salt
1-1/2 teaspoons red
pepper
1/4 teaspoon cayenne
pepper
1 egg (beaten)
1/2 cup plain bread
crumbs

Combine all ingredients in a food processor to thoroughly blend. Form mixture into tiny crawfish balls. Place on a lightly greased baking sheet.

Bake at 375 degrees - 12-15 minutes or until lightly browned and slightly crusty.

GRILLED CHILI-PEPPER SHRIMP

1 pound shrimp [*25-30 count] (peeled & deveined)
1 cup olive oil
1/4 cup red wine vinegar
1 Tablespoon soy sauce
1 Tablespoon dried red chili peppers (crushed)
2 whole green onions (finely chopped)
1 Tablespoon dried parsley
1 garlic clove (minced)

Layer shrimp in a large, glass baking dish.

Combine remaining ingredients to make a marinade. Whisk to blend. Pour marinade over shrimp. Cover and chill several hours or overnight. Grill over medium heat until shrimp turn pink.

Shrimp may also be broiled.

MARINATED SHRIMP

1 pound cooked shrimp (peeled & deveined)
1 onion (sliced into thin rings)
1/2 cup green onion (finely chopped)
1/2 cup black olives
3/4 cup salad oil
1/2 cup white vinegar
1-1/2 Tablespoons sugar
1/2 teaspoon salt
1/4 teaspoon black pepper
1/8 teaspoon red pepper
1/8 teaspoon garlic salt

Layer shrimp in a large, deep bowl. Top with onion rings, greens onions, and olives.

Combine remaining ingredients to make a marinade. Whisk to blend. Pour mixture over shrimp. Marinate 12 - 24 hours.

*25-30 count is the average number of shrimp needed to make I pound

SEAFOOD DIP

1 stick butter
1 bunch green onions (chopped)
1 stalk celery (chopped)
1 (8-ounce) package cream cheese (softened)
1 pound boiled shrimp (chopped)
1 (4.5-ounce) can crabmeat
1 (6.5-ounce) can clams (chopped)
1 (4-ounce) jar sliced mushrooms (drained)
1 (5-ounce) can evaporated milk
1/2 teaspoon Creole seasoning
1/4 teaspoon black pepper

Sauté onions and celery in butter until tender. Remove from heat. Add cream cheese to hot vegetables. Blend well. Remove from heat. Stir in remaining ingredients. Chill several hours for maximum flavor.

CRAB DIP

1 (8-ounce) package cream cheese
1/2 cup sour cream
2 teaspoons horseradish
1 teaspoon Worcestershire sauce
1/2 teaspoon salt
1/4 teaspoon cayenne pepper
1/4 teaspoon paprika
1/2 teaspoon liquid smoke
1 (6-ounce) can crabmeat

Blend cream cheese, sour cream, horseradish, and Worcestershire sauce. Add salt, pepper, and paprika. Stir in liquid smoke and crabmeat. Chill 1-2 hours.

SMOKED SALMON LOG

1 (16-ounce) can salmon

1 (8-ounce) package cream cheese (softened)

1 Tablespoon lemon juice

1 Tablespoon horse-radish

2 Tablespoons finely chopped onion

3/4 teaspoon liquid smoke seasoning

1/4 teaspoon salt

1/8 teaspoon garlic powder

1/2 cup slivered almonds (lightly toasted)

Combine all ingredients, except almonds. Mix thoroughly. Chill at least 2 hours. (More flavorful if made a day before serving.) Shape into slender log-shaped roll. Sprinkle with almonds.

SALMON SPREAD

1 (7-3/4-ounce) can salmon

1 (8-ounce) package cream cheese (softened)

1 (.67-ounce) package Good Seasons Italian seasonings

1 teaspoon hot sauce

1 teaspoon lemon juice

Combine all ingredients. Blend well. Press into a bowl lined with plastic wrap. Chill several hours.

CHICKEN SALAD SPREAD

2 (5-ounce) cans breast of chicken
1 (8-ounce) package cream cheese (softened)
3 Tablespoons whipping cream
1 Tablespoon mayonnaise
1 teaspoon horseradish
1/2 teaspoon salt
1/2 teaspoon white pepper
1/4 teaspoon red pepper
1/8 teaspoon garlic powder
1/2 cup finely chopped green onion
3/4 cup finely chopped pecans (lightly toasted)

Drain chicken and set aside. Whip together cream cheese, whipping cream, mayonnaise, and horseradish. Add seasonings. Stir in chicken, green onion, and pecans. Chill thoroughly before serving.

May also be used as filling for pastry rollups.

DEVILED EGGS

6 large eggs
3 Tablespoons salad dressing
1 Tablespoon sweet pickle relish
2 teaspoons prepared mustard
1/4 teaspoon salt
1/8 teaspoon black pepper
1/8 teaspoon white pepper
1 teaspoon paprika

Cover eggs with water in a large saucepan. Bring water to a rolling boil for five minutes. Turn off heat and cover with a tight-fitting lid for 20 minutes. Peel eggs. Chill 15 minutes.

Cut eggs in half lengthwise and remove yolks. In a small mixing bowl, mash yolks. Add remaining ingredients and mix well. Fill whites with mixture. Sprinkle with paprika. Chill until ready to serve.

LAYERED CHEESE ROLL

1 (8-ounce) package process cheese spread

1 (8-ounce) package jalapēno process cheese spread

1 (8-ounce) package cream cheese (softened)

1/2 large bell pepper (finely chopped)

1 bunch green onions (finely chopped)

1/2 cup ground pecans

Combine cheeses. Divide cheese mixture into two parts. Coat large square of aluminum foil with vegetable spray. Take 1 part of mixture and press into a rectangular shape 1/4-inch thick.

In a small mixing bowl, combine cream cheese, bell pepper, and green onions. Blend until mixture is smooth. Spread 1/2 cream cheese mixture over rolled out cheese. Sprinkle 1/4 cup pecans over mixture. Lift edge of foil to roll into a pinwheel. Shape into a smooth cheese roll. Roll in plastic wrap and cover with foil. Repeat procedure for second portion of cheese roll. Chill overnight.

Cheese rolls may be frozen.

TACO CHEESE DIP

1 (8-ounce) package
cream cheese

1 (8-ounce) carton
sour cream

8 ounces sharp
Cheddar cheese
(grated)

8 ounces Monterrey
Jack cheese
(grated)

1 (1.25-ounce) package
taco seasoning mix

2 teaspoons hot sauce

Heat cheeses and sour cream in a saucepan until mixture is creamy. Stir in taco seasoning and hot sauce. Whisk to blend ingredients.

1/2 pound browned ground beef may be added to make nacho sauce.

Perceval chuckles as he shares childhood experiences that date back to 1932. "The only chance that a young lad had to really do any serious courting was at the monthly church socials. The younger boys and girls gathered around a #3 wash tub for a chance to turn the crank on that old, wooden ice cream churn. There was always plenty of homemade cookies and lemonade to eat while the ice cream was freezing."

ARTICHOKE DIP

1 (14-ounce) can arti-
  choke hearts
  (drained & chopped)

1 (4-ounce) can
  chopped green
  chilies

3/4 cup salad dressing

3/4 cup grated
  Parmesan cheese

2 Tablespoons chopped
  pimiento

Combine all ingredients. Pour into a greased 1-quart baking di

B s - 25 minutes.

GUACAMOLE

2 avocados (peeled &
  mashed)

1 small tomato (peeled
  & chopped)

1/4 cup sour cream

1/4 cup mayonnaise

1/4 cup finely chopped
  onion

1 clove garlic (minced)

2 Tablespoons lemon
  juice

1 (4-ounce) can
  chopped green chili
  peppers

3/4 teaspoon salt

Combine all ingredients in a glass bowl. Cover with plastic wrap. Chill several hours before serving.

HOT SPINACH DIP

1 (10-ounce) package
 frozen chopped
 spinach

1 Tablespoon olive oil

1/2 cup finely chopped
 onion

2 tomatoes (finely
 chopped)

3 Tablespoons chopped
 green chili peppers

1 cup grated Monterrey
 Jack cheese

1 cup cubed process
 cheese

1 (8-ounce) package
 cream cheese
 (softened)

1-1/3 cups half & half

1/4 cup chopped black
 olives

2 Tablespoons white
 wine

1/2 teaspoon salt

1/4 teaspoon black
 pepper

1/4 teaspoon red pepper

Thaw, drain, and place spinach on paper towels to remove excess liquid.

Sauté onion in oil until clear. Add tomatoes. Simmer 3 minutes. In a large mixing bowl, combine sautéed vegetables with remaining ingredients. Mix thoroughly. Pour into a casserole dish.

Bake at 400 degrees 30-40 minutes.

Additional half & half may be added for thinner consistency.

SPICY VEGETABLE DIP

1 (8-ounce) package
   cream cheese
1/4 cup hot chili
   sauce
1 cup sour cream
1/2 teaspoon
   seasoned salt
1/8 teaspoon
   cayenne pepper
1/8 teaspoon garlic
   powder
1 teaspoon dried
   parsley flakes

Combine cream cheese and chili sauce. Beat until creamy. Add remaining ingredients. Blend thoroughly. Chill before serving.

SUN-DRIED TOMATO DIP

1 (7-ounce) package
   sun-dried
   tomatoes
1 clove garlic
   (minced)
1 (8-ounce) package
   cream cheese
   (softened)
2 teaspoons olive oil
1 Tablespoon finely
   chopped jalapeño
   peppers

Cover dried tomatoes in boiling water. Soak for 30 minutes. Drain thoroughly. Remove any hard tough pieces from tomatoes. Blot tomatoes thoroughly with paper towels to remove any excess water. Chop into very small pieces.

In a separate bowl, combine garlic, cream cheese, and olive oil. Blend until creamy. Stir in peppers. Combine both mixtures. Blend until creamy.

FRUIT DIP

1 (8-ounce) package
   cream cheese
   (softened)
3 Tablespoons
   powdered sugar
1/4 cup vanilla yogurt
1/4 teaspoon cinnamon
1/8 teaspoon nutmeg

Combine cream cheese and powdered sugar. Blend until smooth. Stir in yogurt, cinnamon, and nutmeg. Chill.

MARSHMALLOW FRUIT DIP

2 (8-ounce) packages
   cream cheese
   (softened)
1 (7-ounce) jar marshmallow cream
2 teaspoons grated
   lemon peel

Combine all ingredients. Cream mixture. Chill before serving.

One of the most closely guarded places during summer was the watermelon patch. No trespassing was allowed in this area, but somehow every youngster who grew up in the Rural South has a "watermelon stealing" story to tell.

GRANNY'S PARCHED PEANUTS

8 cups unshelled peanuts

Preheat oven to 375 degrees. Cover bottom of 13x9x2-inch pan with 8 cups of unshelled peanuts. Bake on middle rack for 20 minutes. Test for doneness. As soon as thin membrane covering peanut slips off easily, remove from oven. (Peanuts will taste as though additional cooking time is needed until nuts are thoroughly cooled.)

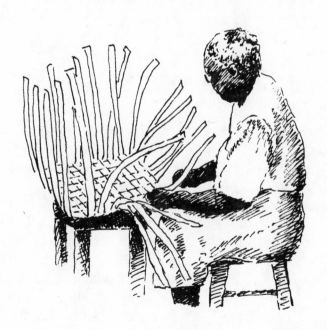

SPICED PECANS

1 egg white
1 Tablespoon apple
   juice
1 teaspoon hot sauce
1 teaspoon water
5 cups pecans
1 cup sugar
1-1/4 teaspoons
   cinnamon
1/2 teaspoon nutmeg
1/2 teaspoon allspice
1/2 teaspoon salt

Whisk egg white, apple juice, hot sauce, and water to blend. Add pecans to mixture. Toss to coat. Let set 10 minutes.

In a separate bowl, combine remaining ingredients. Sprinkle dry mixture over pecans. Mix well. Spread nuts over bottom of a lightly greased 13x9x2-inch baking pan.

Bake at 325 degrees - 20 minutes.

Remove from pan to a sheet of wax paper. Break nuts into small pieces.

ORANGE-FLAVORED WALNUTS

5 cups walnuts
2 cups sugar
3 Tablespoons grated
   orange peel
2/3 cup evaporated
   milk
3 Tablespoons orange
   juice

Combine sugar, orange peel, and milk in a heavy saucepan. Cook mixture, stirring constantly, until liquid reaches soft ball stage. Remove from heat. Continue to stir for 3 minutes. Add orange juice. Beat until mixture becomes cloudy. Stir in walnuts. Continue to stir until mixture begins to turn to a sugary coating. Turn onto a generously buttered pan. After walnuts have cooled slightly, break into small pieces.

CIDER PUNCH

1 quart apple cider
1/2 cup sugar
1 cup orange juice
1/4 cup lemon juice
1 (12-ounce) can
    ginger ale

Heat apple cider and sugar just enough to dissolve sugar. After mixture has cooled thoroughly, add remaining ingredients. Mix well.

SPICED CITRUS TEA

2 quarts boiling water
8 whole cloves
2 (3-inch) cinnamon
    sticks
6 tea bags
1 cup sugar
1 cup orange juice
1/3 cup lemon juice

Heat water to a boiling temperature. Drop cloves and cinnamon into water. Boil 6-8 minutes. Add tea bags and boil for 3-4 additional minutes. Remove from heat. Let tea set 5 minutes. Remove bags from tea. Pour through a sieve to remove cloves and cinnamon. Stir in sugar, orange juice, and lemon juice.

SLUSHY PARTY PUNCH

9 lemons
1 (46-ounce) can pine-
apple juice
3 (.13-ounce) packages
strawberry Kool-Aid
3 (6-ounce) cans
orange juice
concentrate
5 cups sugar

Water

Squeeze lemons and strain seeds
from juice. Add remaining ingredients. Stir to mix thoroughly.

Add enough water to make 2-1/2
gallons of liquid. Freeze punch
until slushy.

GRAPE-LEMONADE PUNCH

1 (32-ounce) bottle
white grape juice
1 (6-ounce) can
frozen lemonade
concentrate
1 (6-ounce) can frozen
limeade
concentrate
2 cups water
1 (2-liter) bottle ginger
ale (chilled)
1 (10-ounce) package
frozen raspberries
(partially thawed)

Combine grape juice, lemonade
concentrate, limeade concentrate, and water. Chill until ready
to serve. Just before serving, stir
in ginger ale and raspberries.

ORANGE SHERBET PUNCH

1 quart pineapple juice
1 (8-ounce) can frozen
   lemonade
1 quart orange soda
1/2 gallon orange
   sherbet (slightly
   softened)
1 quart 7-UP

Chill liquid ingredients. Pour pineapple juice, lemonade, and orange soda into a punch bowl.

Just before serving, add a block of sherbet to mixture. Slowly pour 7-UP over sherbet.

RASPBERRY SHERBET PUNCH

1 (6-ounce) can frozen
   pink lemonade
   (thawed)
2 quarts ginger ale
   (chilled)
2 quarts raspberry
   sherbet

Combine lemonade and ginger ale. Mix thoroughly. Add sherbet to a chilled punch bowl. Immediately before serving, pour lemonade mixture over slightly softened sherbet.

SOUTHERN COFFEE PUNCH

1 quart strongly
   brewed coffee
1/3 cup sugar
2 cups chocolate milk
1-1/2 teaspoons
   vanilla extract
1 pint coffee ice
   cream
1 pint vanilla ice
   cream
1 (8-ounce) carton
   whipping cream

Dissolve sugar in hot coffee. Chill thoroughly.

Pour chocolate milk and vanilla into chilled punch bowl. Pour coffee into bowl. Mix thoroughly. Add scoops of ice cream to bowl.

Whip cream to form stiff peaks. Top coffee punch with dollops of whipped cream.

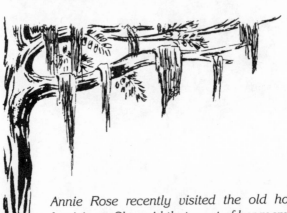

Annie Rose recently visited the old home place in South Louisiana. She said that most of her memories from childhood were centered around Mama working in the kitchen to keep "food on the table" for a family of nine. "As soon as one meal was over, pots were filled and put back on the wood stove for the next meal. We had an ice box until 1947. I remember a standing rule that none of the 'kids' could open the ice box without permission because at two cents a pound, ice was just too expensive to waste."

**breads
brunch**

Summer days in the South were humid, hot and, in general, miserable. After supper and a cooling bath in the old wash tub, each family member made his way to the front porch, hoping for a refreshing breeze to descend and bring an end to the day's punishing heat.

In the dusk, birds were frantically searching for a last few morsels of food before heading to roost. Chickens were slowly moving closer to the hen house, reluctant to stop their scratching and pecking. It was the last few minutes of daylight, and an inky blackness was gradually replacing the amber glow of sunset. Ghost-like shadows danced across the yard as the flickering glow from a single kerosene lamp in the window penetrated the darkness. Faint chirps of crickets from under the steps and the screech of a distant owl signaled all creatures of the night to come alive. Sounds, some old and recognized and some new and unexplained, blended in harmony to add to the mystery of night. Suddenly an unspoken summoning to bed came as the whisper of a gentle breeze spread a hush over the countryside. The now-eerie silence was broken only by the scraping of chairs as each shuffled off to bed.

breads and brunch

buttermilk loaf bread, **36**
country yeast biscuits, **37**
biscuit rolls /quick buttermilk biscuits, **38**
sweet milk biscuits / biscuit variations, **39**
cheese sausage biscuits, **40**
crawfish cornbread / gran's oyster fritters, **41**
southern jalapeño hushpuppies, **42**
down-home cornbread / cheddar spoon bread, **43**
apricot almond bread, **44**
sticky buns, **45**
cinnamon coffee cake, **46**
granny's gingerbread / lawtel gingerbread, **47**
lemon tea bread, **48**
strawberry-lemon poppy seed bread, **49**
pecan date loaf, **50**
basic muffin batter / muffin variations, **51**
peachy walnut muffins, **52**
strawberry muffins, **53**
sweet potato muffins, **54**
brunch casserole, **55**
breakfast pie / cheese grits, **56**
apple sausage ring / sausage pepper roll, **57**
blueberry pancakes / cream cheese pancakes, **58**
cinnamon cream french toast, **59**
apple fritters / basic fritter batter, **60**
country fried apples, **61**
breakfast toppers, **62**

BUTTERMILK LOAF BREAD

2 cups buttermilk
2 (1.4-ounce) pack-
   ages yeast
4 Tablespoons sugar
3 teaspoons salt
5 cups all-purpose
   flour
1 Tablespoon melted
   shortening
1 Tablespoon melted
   butter
2 Tablespoons
   vegetable oil

Heat buttermilk until a boiling bubble breaks the surface. Cool to lukewarm (approximately 110 degrees). Add yeast to buttermilk. Let set 10 minutes. Add sugar and salt. Stir in 2 cups flour. Beat until smooth. Add remaining flour (or enough to make a soft dough.) Add shortening and butter. Knead dough until smooth and elastic. Coat surface of dough with vegetable oil. Place dough in a generously greased bowl. Cover with a damp cloth and set in a warm, draft-free area. Let dough rise until doubled in size (approximately 1-1/2 hours). Punch down and knead several times until dough is smooth. Place in (2) 8-inch greased loaf pans. Cover and let rise until doubled in bulk (approximately 1 hour).

Bake at 425 degrees 10 minutes, then reduce heat to 350 degrees. Bake additional 20 minutes. Cover with aluminum foil if top browns too rapidly.

Brush top with additional melted butter after bread is removed from oven.

COUNTRY YEAST BISCUITS

2-1/2 cups all-purpose
   flour
1-1/2 teaspoons baking
   powder
1-1/4 teaspoons salt
1/2 teaspoon soda
4 Tablespoons sugar
1/2 cup shortening
1/4 cup lukewarm water
1 (1.4-ounce) package
   yeast
1 cup buttermilk
3 Tablespoons butter

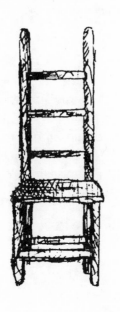

Sift dry ingredients. Cut shortening into mixture with pastry blender or fork until crumbly.

In a small dish, dissolve yeast in lukewarm water (100 degrees). Add buttermilk to dissolved yeast after mixture has thoroughly cooled. Pour buttermilk mixture into a large mixing bowl. Gradually add dry ingredients, mixing lightly after each addition. Dough will be very soft and sticky. Turn onto floured board. Knead until dough is smooth and elastic. (Approximately 5 minutes.) Additional flour (no more than 1/2 cup) may be used while kneading.

Pinch off 2-inch pieces. Roll between palms (sprinkled with flour) to smooth, then lightly flatten to 1-1/2-inch thickness. Place in a greased 10-inch iron skillet. Place biscuits close together, starting with center biscuit and working outward. Pat down lightly so that all biscuits are the same height.

Melt butter and brush over entire surface of dough. Cover with slightly damp cloth. Let rise 1-2 hours or until doubled in size.

Bake at 375 degrees 15-18 minutes or until lightly browned.

BISCUIT ROLLS

2 cups biscuit mix
2 teaspoons sugar
1 (8-ounce) carton sour
    cream
1 stick butter (melted)

Combine dry ingredients. Add sour cream and butter. Beat to blend. Drop dough from a Tablespoon onto a generously floured surface. Roll into a smooth ball. Place 3 balls into each well of a greased muffin tin.

Bake at 350 degrees 18-20 minutes.

QUICK BUTTERMILK BISCUITS

2 cups self-rising flour
1/2 cup shortening
1 cup buttermilk

Cut shortening into flour. Gradually add buttermilk. Stir to blend thoroughly. Knead dough 10-12 times on a lightly floured surface. Pinch off small pieces of dough. Shape into biscuits and flatten slightly. Arrange in a generously greased skillet.

Bake at 400 degrees 15-20 minutes or until golden brown.

*SWEET MILK BISCUITS

**2 cups all-purpose flour
1 Tablespoon baking
   powder
1 teaspoon salt
5 Tablespoons shortening
3/4 cup sweet milk**

Sift dry ingredients. Cut shortening into mixture with a pastry cutter or fork to evenly distribute shortening. (Mixture will resemble coarse cornmeal.)

Pour milk into mixture. Stir as little as possible to make a soft dough. Turn dough onto floured wax paper. Knead gently to count of 20. (Dough should be smooth on surface.) Pat out to 1/2-inch thickness. Cut with a sharp, floured 2-inch cutter. Place biscuits in a greased 10-inch skillet. Start in center and place biscuits so that they touch each other.

Bake at 400 degrees 15-20 minutes or until golden brown.

BISCUIT VARIATIONS

CHEESE PINWHEELS - Roll dough to a rectangular shape approximately 1/4-inch in thickness. Spread with 4 Tablespoons softened process cheese. Sprinkle with 1/2 cup grated Cheddar cheese. Roll up jelly-roll style. Cut crosswise into 3/4 inch thick slices. Place on a generously greased baking sheet. Cut side of biscuit should be facing downward. Brush with 3 Tablespoons melted butter. Loosely cover with foil if cheese begins to become too brown on biscuit tops.

ORANGE TEA BISCUITS - Add 1 Tablespoon grated orange peel to flour and shortening mixture. Add 1 Tablespoon orange juice to milk. Roll dough out to 1/2-inch thickness. Cut with a small biscuit cutter. Press sugar cube soaked in orange juice into center of dough. Press all the way into dough.

BUTTERMILK BISCUITS - Substitute 3/4 cup buttermilk for sweet milk. Decrease baking powder to 1-1/2 teaspoons. Add 1 teaspoon soda to buttermilk. Let set 5 minutes.

---

* This term distinguishes regular milk from buttermilk. Some "old-timers" still use this reference to identify milk.

CHEESE SAUSAGE BISCUITS

1 pound hot ground
  sausage
2 cups Bisquick all-
  purpose baking mix
2/3 cup milk
1 Tablespoon drippings
  from sausage
2 teaspoons sugar
1 cup grated Cheddar
  cheese
1/2 stick melted butter

Brown sausage in a skillet until crumbly. Drain excess drippings, reserving 1 Tablespoon for later use. Blot sausage with paper towels.

In a separate bowl, sift baking mix. Stir in milk, reserved drippings, sugar, and cheese. Mixture will make a soft dough. Turn onto a lightly floured cutting board. Knead only enough to give shape to dough. Pinch off small pieces of dough and shape in a round ball. Pat to flatten slightly. Place in a greased skillet so that biscuits touch. Brush melted butter over biscuits.

Bake at 400 degrees 5 minutes. Reduce heat to 375 degrees. Bake additional 7-10 minutes or until lightly browned.

Tappey Boy remembers coming home after school and racing into the kitchen for a leftover biscuit. He would poke a hole in the top of the biscuit and fill it with homemade cane syrup.

CRAWFISH CORNBREAD

1 cup yellow cornmeal
1/3 cup cooking oil
1 teaspoon salt
1/2 teaspoon baking
    soda
1 (15-1/4-ounce) can
    cream-style corn
2 eggs
1/2 pound grated
    Cheddar cheese
1 cup finely chopped
    onion
1 pound crawfish tails

Mix all ingredients, except crawfish, in order listed. Blend until mixture is moist.

Stir in crawfish tails. Pour into a 9x12-inch greased baking dish.

Bake at 375 degrees - 30 minutes.

GRAN'S OYSTER FRITTERS

2 pints fresh oysters
    (drained)
1/4 cup green onion
    (finely chopped)
1 teaspoon paprika
1 cup yellow cornmeal
1 cup all-purpose flour
2 teaspoons baking
    powder
1 teaspoon salt
1/4 teaspoon cayenne
    pepper
2 eggs
1/4 cup sour cream
1 teaspoon hot sauce
1/2 cup buttermilk

Cut each oyster into 4 pieces. Combine oysters and green onions in a mixing bowl. Sprinkle with paprika and set aside.

Sift all dry ingredients.

In a separate bowl, combine eggs, sour cream, hot sauce, and buttermilk. Whisk to blend thoroughly. Stir into dry mixture (a small portion at a time). Fold oysters and onion into batter. Drop from Tablespoon into hot oil. Fry until golden brown.

SOUTHERN JALAPEÑO HUSHPUPPIES

1 cup self-rising cornmeal
1/2 cup self-rising flour
1/2 teaspoon sugar
1/2 teaspoon salt
1/4 teaspoon sage
1 small onion (finely chopped)
3 whole green onions (finely chopped)
2 Tablespoons (finely chopped) jalapeño peppers
1/2 cup whole kernel corn (drained)
1 egg
3/4 cup milk

Combine dry ingredients with onions, jalapeño peppers, and corn.

Beat egg until creamy. Stir egg into mixture. Gradually add milk, (Amount of milk may vary.) Let mixture set 10 minutes. Mixture should be thick enough to drop from teaspoon to form 1-inch balls. Deep fry in hot fat (375 degrees) until lightly browned (usually 3-4 minutes).

When Reverend Johnson came to our house to have Sunday dinner, Mama would serve fried chicken, fried corn, dirty rice, potato salad, cabbage "greens," pigs feet, and apple pie. Daddy, who was the cornbread specialist, would make a large pone of bread in his prized cast-iron skillet. He also made cornbread muffins and cornbread sticks. The preacher would eat heartily and say that we were all blessed to be healthy and eatin' so "high on the hog."

DOWN-HOME CORNBREAD

1 cup yellow cornmeal
1 cup all-purpose flour
2 Tablespoons sugar
1 Tablespoon baking powder
1/2 teaspoon salt
1-3/4 cups milk
1 egg (slightly beaten)
3 Tablespoons cooking oil

Combine all ingredients. Beat at least 15 strokes to mix well. Pour into a generously greased 10-inch skillet.

Bake at 425 degrees 20-25 minutes.

Bread flour may be used as a substitute for all-purpose flour.

CHEDDAR SPOON BREAD

2 cups milk
1/2 cup yellow cornmeal
1 cup grated sharp Cheddar cheese
4 Tablespoons butter
2 teaspoons sugar
1 teaspoon salt
2 eggs (beaten)

Heat 1-1/2 cups milk until first boiling bubble breaks surface. Remove from heat. In a small mixing bowl, combine 1/2 cup remaining milk and cornmeal. Stir mixture into hot milk. Combine cornmeal, cheese, butter, sugar, and salt to mixture. Cook on low heat until slightly thickened. Remove from heat. Pour beaten eggs, a small amount at a time, into cornmeal mixture. Whisk while adding eggs. Pour into 1-quart greased baking dish.

Bake at 350 degrees - 35 minutes or until knife comes out clean when inserted into center.

APRICOT ALMOND BREAD

1 cup dried apricots
(chopped)
1 cup sugar
1/2 cup butter
3 eggs
3/4 cup orange juice
1/4 cup sour cream
1/2 teaspoon almond
extract
2 cups all-purpose flour
1 teaspoon salt
3 teaspoons baking
powder
1/2 teaspoon baking
soda
1 cup sliced almonds
(toasted)

Plump apricots by soaking in warm water five minutes. Remove apricots from water and drain. Place on paper towels to remove excess liquid.

Beat sugar and butter until creamy. Add eggs, orange juice, sour cream, and almond extract. Whisk until blended thoroughly.

In a separate bowl, sift dry ingredients. Add creamy mixture to flour. Fold apricots and almonds into batter.

Bake at 350 degrees 1 hour 10 minutes.

STICKY BUNS

24 frozen dinner rolls
2/3 cup granulated
   sugar
2 teaspoons cinnamon
3/4 cup chopped
   pecans
2/3 cup brown sugar
1/2 cup butter (cut into
   16 pieces)
1 (4-ounce) package
   butterscotch
   pudding mix
   (non-instant)

Place a layer of frozen rolls in a greased bundt cake pan.

Combine sugar and cinnamon. Sprinkle a portion of mixture over rolls. Make a layer of chopped nuts, brown sugar, and pudding mix over rolls. Place slices of butter around rolls. Repeat procedure until all rolls and toppings have been used. Cover pan with a slightly damp cloth. Let set overnight in warm, draft-free area.

Bake at 350 degrees 35-40 minutes. Remove from oven and turn pan upside down over serving tray. Wait 10 minutes before lifting pan.

Mr. Allen lived in the same community his entire life. He related the following story. "I walked three miles to work six days a week. My wife always had hot biscuits, homemade syrup, and bacon cured in the smokehouse ready for breakfast. She would pack the leftovers in a syrup bucket. I had to be on the job at 6:00 a.m. The work day ended when there was no more daylight. I made 50 cents a day and felt lucky to earn that. After working for almost a year, my wages were doubled because I was such a good worker."

CINNAMON COFFEE CAKE

2 sticks butter
  (softened)

1 cup granulated sugar

1 cup brown sugar
  (firmly packed)

1 (3-ounce) package
  cream cheese

2 eggs

3/4 cup sour cream

1 teaspoon vanilla
  extract

2 cups all-purpose
  flour

1 teaspoon baking
  powder

1/2 teaspoon baking
  soda

1/4 teaspoon salt

I teaspoon cinnamon

Cream butter, sugars, and cream cheese. Beat in eggs, sour cream, and vanilla. Sift remaining dry ingredients. Add to sour cream mixture. Pour 1/2 batter into a greased 9-inch tube pan.

TOPPING

2 Tablespoons brown
  sugar

1 Tablespoon butter
  (softened)

1 cup chopped pecans
  (lightly toasted)

1 teaspoon cinnamon

Combine all topping ingredients to make a crumbly mixture. Sprinkle 1/2 mixture over batter. Pour remaining batter over topping. Sprinkle with remaining mixture.

Bake at 350 degrees - 50-60 minutes.

GRANNY'S GINGERBREAD

1/2 cup shortening
2/3 cup sugar
1 cup molasses
2 teaspoons cinnamon
1/2 teaspoon ginger
1/2 teaspoon ground cloves
3/4 teaspoon salt
2-1/2 cups all-purpose flour
2 teaspoons soda
1 cup boiling water
2 eggs (beaten)

Cream shortening. Add sugar 2 Tablespoons at a time, beating after each addition. Stir in molasses, cinnamon, ginger, cloves, and salt. Add flour and mix thoroughly. Add soda to boiling water. Gradually pour into mixture while beating with electric mixer. Add eggs and continue to beat until well blended. Pour into a greased 15x10x1-inch baking pan. (Batter will be very thin.)

Bake at 350 degrees 35-40 minutes.

LAWTEL GINGERBREAD

2 cups all-purpose flour
1-1/2 teaspoons baking soda
1/2 teaspoon salt
2 teaspoons cinnamon
1 teaspoon allspice
1 teaspoon ginger
1-1/2 cups brown sugar (firmly packed)
1/2 cup molasses
1/4 cup butter (softened)
2 eggs (beaten)
1 cup milk
1 cup chopped pecans (lightly toasted)

Sift flour, baking soda, salt, and spices.

Combine brown sugar, molasses, butter, and eggs. Beat to blend. Alternately add dry ingredients and milk to flour mixture, beating after each addition. Fold in nuts. Pour mixture into a greased and floured 9x5x2-inch loaf pan. Sprinkle with nuts.

Bake at 350 degrees 30 minutes.

LEMON TEA BREAD

1 stick butter
1 cup sugar
2 eggs
1-1/2 cups all-purpose
   flour
1/2 teaspoon baking
   powder
1/2 teaspoon baking
   soda
1/2 cup buttermilk
3 Tablespoons squeezed
   lemon juice
2 teaspoons lemon peel

Cream butter and sugar until fluffy. Beat eggs into mixture.

Sift dry ingredients. Alternately add dry ingredients and buttermilk to creamed mixture. Stir in lemon juice and peel. Beat vigorously. Pour batter into a greased and lightly floured 9x5x2-inch loaf pan.

Bake at 325 degrees 35-40 minutes.

To make a glaze, combine 1-3/4 cups powdered sugar and 3 Tablespoons fresh lemon juice. Pour glaze over loaf.

Some things just are - no reason, no explanation - they just are. The "bottle tree", observed in isolated southern communities in the 30's and 40's, was such a mystery. The trees come in all varieties. They had bottles and jars hanging from every bough. There was one adorned with only blue bottles. When Mr. Johnson was asked about his bottle tree, he shrugged and said, "It's been here as long as I can remember, and I just keep adding and replacing bottles."

STRAWBERRY-LEMON POPPY SEED BREAD

1/4 cup sugar
2 eggs
1 (7-ounce) package strawberry muffin mix w/strawberries
1/2 cup milk
1/2 cup vegetable oil
2 Tablespoons lemon juice
2-1/2 Tablespoons poppy seeds

Combine sugar and eggs, Blend thoroughly. Stir in muffin mix. Alternately add milk and oil, mixing after each addition. Fold in lemon juice, poppy seeds, and strawberries. Pour into a greased and floured 8-inch loaf pan.

Bake at 350 degrees 35-45 minutes or until toothpick comes clean when inserted into loaf.

To make a glaze, combine 3/4 cup powdered sugar and 1 Tablespoon lemon juice. Mix ingredients thoroughly. Drizzle over warm bread.

PECAN DATE LOAF

4 eggs
1 cup cooking oil
2 cups sugar
1 teaspoon vanilla
   extract
1 teaspoon butter
   extract
1 teaspoon rum extract
1 cup buttermilk
2 cups all-purpose
   flour
1 teaspoon baking
   soda
1 teaspoon cinnamon
1/2 teaspoon allspice
1/2 teaspoon nutmeg
1/2 teaspoon salt
3/4 cup chopped dates
2 cups chopped
   pecans

In a large bowl, beat eggs until creamy. Add oil, sugar, extracts, and buttermilk. Beat until blended.

In a separate bowl, sift dry ingredients and gradually add to mixture. Fold in dates and pecans. Pour batter into a 9-inch greased and lightly floured loaf pan.

Bake at 325 degrees 1 hour 10 minutes.

Test for doneness in center of loaf with a long thin wooden skewer. This rich bread will bake much slower in center of loaf.

BASIC MUFFIN BATTER

2 cups sifted all-purpose flour
2 teaspoons baking powder
3/4 teaspoon salt
2/3 cup sugar
2 eggs (slightly beaten)
1 cup milk
1/3 cup vegetable oil

All ingredients should be at room temperature. Measure flour after sifting. Add remaining dry ingredients. Combine liquid ingredients. Stir only enough to moisten mixture. (Do not over beat. Mixture should be lumpy.) Grease only the bottom of each muffin well for increased volume. Fill muffin tins 1/2 full.

Bake at 375 degrees 18-20 minutes.

MUFFIN VARIATIONS

BLUEBERRY MUFFINS: Add 1 cup fresh or frozen blueberries to dry ingredients. Add additional 2 Tablespoons sugar and 1 teaspoon lemon juice.

CHERRY MUFFINS: Add 3/4 cup dried cherries and 1 Tablespoon sugar to muffin batter.

HALF-IN, HALF-OUT MUFFINS: Combine 1/2 cup firmly packed brown sugar, 2 teaspoons cinnamon, 1/4 teaspoon nutmeg, 3/4 cup finely chopped toasted pecans, and 3 Tablespoons melted butter. Add 1/2 mixture to recipe for basic muffins. Mix thoroughly. Fill muffin tins 1/2 full. Sprinkle remaining brown sugar mixture over muffins.

PEACHY WALNUT MUFFINS

1 stick butter (softened)
1/2 cup granulated sugar
1/2 cup brown sugar
2 eggs
3/4 cup milk
1/4 cup orange juice
1 teaspoon vanilla extract
1/4 cup quick rolled oats
2 cups all-purpose flour
2 teaspoons baking
   powder
1/4 teaspoon salt
1 teaspoon cinnamon
3 cup chopped peaches

Blend butter and sugars until mixture is creamy. In a separate bowl, beat eggs, milk, orange juice, and vanilla. Add to butter mixture. Stir in oats. Sift remaining dry ingredients. Add to liquid mixture. Mix just enough to blend. Fold in peaches. Spoon mixture into greased muffin tin wells. Fill 2/3 full.

TOPPING

1/4 cup sugar
3/4 cup walnuts (finely
   chopped)
2 Tablespoons butter

Combine sugar, walnuts, and butter. Spoon 1 teaspoon topping over unbaked muffins.

Bake at 325 degrees 20-25 minutes.

STRAWBERRY MUFFINS

2-1/2 cups all-purpose flour

1 cup sugar

2 teaspoons baking powder

1 teaspoon baking soda

3/4 teaspoon salt

3/4 cup buttermilk

1/4 cup orange juice

2 eggs (slightly beaten)

1/3 cup vegetable oil

1-1/2 cups fresh strawberries (thinly sliced)

1/2 cup strawberry jam

1 teaspoon cinnamon

1/2 teaspoon ginger

1/4 teaspoon nutmeg

Sift flour, sugar, baking powder, baking soda, and salt together. In a separate bowl, combine buttermilk, orange juice, eggs, and oil. Combine both mixtures. Stir until mixture is moistened.

Fold in strawberries. (If frozen strawberries are used, drain thoroughly and blot excess liquid with paper towels.) Mix to blend. (Do not over mix batter). Fill greased muffin tins 1/2 full. Spoon 1/2 teaspoon jam over batter.

Combine spices. Sprinkle spices over batter. Add remaining batter to fill each tin 2/3 full.

Bake 375 degrees 20 minutes.

Prof, who now lives in Central Louisiana, recalls long hot summer months in Mississippi. "I spent a lot of time with Mama Bea, my grandmother. On Saturday afternoon, we would walk along the tracks to get to the general store in Clarksdale. Once inside, she would reach into her bosom and pull out a white handkerchief tied in a small neat knot. She always had enough money to buy two RC Colas. Mama Bea earned this money by picking cotton on a nearby farm."

SWEET POTATO MUFFINS

1/2 cup butter
(softened)
1 cup granulated sugar
1/4 cup brown sugar
2 large eggs (beaten)
1-1/2 cups mashed
sweet potatoes
1-1/2 cups all-purpose
flour
2 teaspoons baking
powder
1 teaspoon salt
1-1/2 teaspoons
cinnamon
1/2 teaspoon nutmeg
1 cup milk
1/2 cup raisins
1/2 cups chopped
pecans (lightly
toasted)

Cream butter and sugars. Stir in eggs and sweet potatoes. Beat to blend thoroughly.

Sift all dry ingredients. Alternately stir dry ingredients and milk into sweet potato mixture. Stir only to blend thoroughly. Fold in raisins and nuts.

Bake at 400 degrees 25 minutes.

BRUNCH CASSEROLE

1 pound ground
   sausage
16 slices white bread
   (crust removed)
1-1/4 cups grated
   Cheddar cheese
6 eggs (beaten)
1 teaspoon salt
1 teaspoon pepper
1 teaspoon
   Worcestershire
   sauce
3 cups milk
3 Tablespoons minced
   onion
3 Tablespoons finely
   chopped bell
   pepper

Brown sausage in a skillet. Drain meat and blot with paper towels. Place 8 slices of bread in a greased 13x9x2-inch baking dish. Sprinkle 1/2 sausage and 1/2 cheese over bread. Layer remaining 8 slices of bread over cheese and sausage.

In a large mixing bowl, combine remaining ingredients. Whisk vigorously until mixture is blended. Pour egg mixture over bread slices. Sprinkle remaining sausage first, then cheese. Refrigerate casserole overnight.

Bake at 350 degrees 50-60 minutes.

BREAKFAST PIE

1/2 pound ground
   sausage
1 (9-inch deep dish)
   unbaked pie crust
1 (4-ounce) can green
   chilies
1-1/2 cups grated
   Monterey Jack cheese
1 Tablespoon all-purpose
   flour
3 eggs
1 cup half & half
1 teaspoon salt
1 teaspoon pepper
1/2 teaspoon chili powder

Brown sausage. Drain excess grease.

Layer chilies in bottom of pie crust. Toss cheese with flour. Top chilies with 1/2 grated cheese. Make a layer of sausage. Top with remaining cheese.

In a small bowl, combine eggs, milk, and seasonings. Whisk until thoroughly blended. Pour over mixture in pie crust.

Bake at 350 degrees 40-45 minutes or until knife comes out clean.

CHEESE GRITS

1 cup uncooked grits
1/3 cup butter (melted)
3 eggs (beaten)
1/4 cup milk
8 ounces Cheddar cheese
   (grated)
1 teaspoon hot sauce
1/4 teaspoon garlic
   powder

Cook grits according to package directions.

Combine remaining ingredients. Whisk to blend thoroughly. Pour mixture into hot grits. Stir to mix. Pour into a greased casserole dish.

Bake at 325 degrees 55 minutes or until set.

APPLE SAUSAGE RING

2 pounds ground pork
   sausage
2 cups plain bread
   crumbs
2 eggs (beaten)
3/4 cup evaporated milk
3 Tablespoons minced
   onion
2 teaspoons sugar
1 large apple (finely
   chopped)

Combine ingredients. Mix well. Line a 2-quart bundt pan with plastic wrap coated with vegetable spray. Press mixture into pan to shape. Chill 15-20 minutes. Turn packed mixture into a glass baking dish. Remove plastic wrap.

Bake at 350 degrees 50-60 minutes.

Apple sausage ring may be partially baked a day ahead of time.

SAUSAGE PEPPER ROLL

2 (16-ounce) loaves
   frozen bread dough
1/2 pound pork sausage
1/2 pound ground beef
1/2 cup finely chopped
   onion
1/4 cup finely chopped
   bell pepper
2 Tablespoons finely
   chopped jalapeño
   peppers
1-1/2 cups grated
   Cheddar cheese
1 cup grated Monterey
   Jack cheese
2 Tablespoons melted
   butter

Thaw bread loaves. Roll each loaf out on a floured surface to form a 9x16-inch rectangular shape. Place on greased baking sheets.

Cook sausage, ground beef, onion, bell pepper, and jalapeño peppers in a large skillet until meat is browned and vegetables are tender. Drain mixture. Spread 1/2 mixture over each bread rectangle, leaving a 1/2-inch border. Sprinkle with cheeses. Roll up jelly-roll style, starting from 16-inch side. Brush surface with melted butter. Lay seam side down on greased sheets.

Bake at 350 degrees 40 minutes or until golden brown.

BLUEBERRY PANCAKES

1 cup fresh blueberries
1-1/2 cups all-purpose
  flour
1 teaspoon baking
  powder
1/2 teaspoon baking soda
1/2 teaspoon salt
4 Tablespoons powdered
  sugar
1 cup buttermilk
2 eggs
4 Tablespoons butter
  (melted)
1/4 cup rolled oats

Dredge blueberries in 1/2 cup flour. Chill until ready to fold into pancake mixture. Sift 1 cup flour, baking powder, baking soda, salt, and powdered sugar.

In a separate bowl, combine buttermilk, eggs, and butter. Whisk to blend. Add dry ingredients and oats. Mix thoroughly. (Do not over-beat.) Fold in blueberries. Pour 1/3 cup batter onto medium hot, lightly greased griddle. Do not flatten pancakes while cooking.

CREAM CHEESE PANCAKES

1 (5-1/2-ounce) package
  pancake mix
1 teaspoon sugar
1 egg
1 (3-ounce) package
  cream cheese
  (softened)
1 Tablespoon margarine
  (melted)
1 cup milk
1 teaspoon vanilla extract

Combine dry ingredients. In a separate bowl. Whip egg, cream cheese, and margarine together. Add to dry ingredients. Stir in milk and vanilla. Beat until all ingredients are blended.

Pour 1/4 cup batter onto hot, lightly greased griddle. Do not press down on tops of pancakes while cooking.

CINNAMON CREAM FRENCH TOAST

8 slices bread (slightly stale)
1 (3-ounce) package cream cheese (softened)
2 teaspoons cinnamon
2 cups milk
2 eggs
2 Tablespoons brown sugar
1 Tablespoon butter

Beat cream cheese and 1 teaspoon cinnamon until soft and creamy. Spread a thin layer of mixture over 4 bread slices. (Spread mixture to edges.) Top with remaining bread. Cut bread in half. In a large mixing bowl, combine I teaspoon cinnamon, milk, eggs, and brown sugar. Whisk until foamy. Leave bread in mixture long enough to thoroughly soak through bread.

Place bread on hot, lightly greased griddle. (Griddle should be preheated so that toast will "seal over" quickly.) Cook over medium heat. Turn several times to avoid a soggy center. Lightly coat with a small pat of butter after removing from griddle.

Drizzle syrup over toast or serve plain.

APPLE FRITTERS

1 cup all-purpose flour
4 Tablespoons sugar
1/2 teaspoon salt
1 teaspoon cinnamon
2 eggs (beaten)
1/2 cup milk
1-1/2 cups apples
  (pared & chopped)
1/3 cup powdered sugar

Sift flour before measuring. Combine sifted flour with sugar, salt, and cinnamon. Beat eggs and milk together. Add to flour mixture. Beat to blend. Fold apples into fritter batter. Drop from teaspoon into deep fat (365 degrees). Fry until evenly browned. Drain on paper towels.

Sprinkle with powdered sugar.

BASIC FRITTER BATTER

1 cup all-purpose flour
2 Tablespoons sugar
1/2 teaspoon salt
2 eggs (well beaten)
1/2 cup milk

Sift flour before measuring. Sift flour a second time with sugar and salt. Beat eggs and milk together until frothy. Add to dry ingredients. Mix until smooth.

Batter may be used with a variety of fruit. The amount of sugar may be adjusted depending on sweetness of fruit. May also be used for chicken or seafood.

COUNTRY FRIED APPLES

3 apples
1/4 cup butter
1/2 cup sugar
1 teaspoon cinnamon
1/4 teaspoon nutmeg

Peel and core apples. Slice lengthwise into 1/2-inch wedges.

Melt butter in a heavy cast-iron skillet. When butter is bubbly, add apple slices. In a mixing bowl, combine sugar, cinnamon, and nutmeg. Sprinkle 1/2 mixture over apples. Simmer over medium heat for 7 minutes. Turn apples and sprinkle with remaining sugar mixture. Baste with liquid while cooking. Apples should be tender, but slightly crunchy.

BREAKFAST TOPPERS

Apple Butter - Combine 4 cups unsweetened applesauce, 1/2 cup sugar, 1 Tablespoon butter, 1 teaspoon lemon juice, 2 teaspoons cinnamon, 1/2 teaspoon allspice, and 1/4 teaspoon nutmeg in a medium saucepan. Bring mixture to a light boil. Simmer over low heat for 20 minutes.

Peach Blossom Cream Cheese Spread - Combine 3/4 cup peach preserves, 1 teaspoon creamy horseradish, 1/2 teaspoon cinnamon, 1/8 teaspoon nutmeg, and 1 (8-ounce) package softened cream cheese. Blend thoroughly. (Excellent with graham crackers, gingersnaps, or bagels.)

Pear Honey - Pare and core 5 large pears. Cut pears into small cubes. Combine pears, 1 cup crushed pineapple, the juice and grated rind from a large lemon, and I Tablespoon ginger in a heavy pot. Bring mixture to a rolling boil. Cover and simmer over low heat 30-40 minutes. (May be cooked longer for thicker consistency.) Stir mixture frequently to prevent sticking. Fruit will become transparent and liquid will thicken. Allow mixture to cool. Store in airtight containers in refrigerator.

Strawberry Preserves - Combine 4 cups fresh crushed strawberries and 3 Tablespoons freshly squeezed lemon juice in a heavy pot. Bring mixture to a rolling boil for 2 minutes, stirring constantly. Let stand 2-3 hours. Ladle cooled preserves into small jelly jars. Keep refrigerated in sealed jars.

Papa's Chocolate Gravy - Combine 2 Tablespoons cocoa, 4 Tablespoons sugar, 1-1/2 Tablespoons all-purpose flour, and 1-1/2 cups milk in a quart jar with tight fitting lid. Shake vigorously until blended. Pour mixture into skillet. Cook over medium heat until "gravy" thickens. Serve over hot biscuits

soups
salads

*T*hin tendril-like swirls of gray smoke rose from the chimney only to be caught in the grasp of a brisk north wind and whisked away. The rustle of drying leaves and the pungent fragrance of burning red oak firewood were lingering evidence that a change was in the air.

Out of sight, high above darkening clouds, the mournful beckoning of geese echoed across barren fields as they journeyed south. The unusual crispness and chill of late evening could only mean one thing; winter had arrived. Extra firewood would be needed tonight.

After supper, everyone retired to the living room and took a favored spot around the fireplace. Papa, as always, was in the creaking old rocker with hands stretched out toward the warm fire as he gazed into the burning embers. And Mama, whose chores never seemed to end, mended a tear in an already-ragged pair of overalls. Casual conversation slowly drifted into silence, broken only by the crackling of the roaring fire and the glow of a spark as it spewed from the fireplace and burned away on the hearth. As dusk deepened into night, the deafening silence of darkness was broken only by the distant bark of a dog and the quarreling of a grumpy old hen changing positions on the roosting pole.

soups and salads

sausage and vegetable soup, **66**

all-american soup, **67**

country vegetable soup / easy chicken noodle soup, **68**

corn and tomato soup, **69**

renna's corn and potato soup, **70**

ham, broccoli, and cheese soup, **71**

chunky potato soup, **72**

cream of squash soup / cream of turnip soup, **73**

cream of tomato soup, **74**

harvest soup, **75**

cucumber and tomato salad, **76**

tossed corn and hominy salad, **77**

sweet and sour cabbage slaw / wilted salad, **78**

carrot and raisin slaw / cabbage and apple slaw, **79**

potato salad, **80**

marinated rice salad / "sweet pea" salad, **81**

louisiana shrimp slaw, **82**

bayou salad / deluxe tuna salad, **83**

macaroni and ham salad, **84**

pasta salad, **85**

strawberry salad, **86**

fresh fruit salad, **87**

tutti-frutti dessert salad / frozen fruit dessert salad, **88**

apple and pear salad, **89**

grammy's ambrosia/ cranberry relish, **90**

SAUSAGE AND VEGETABLE SOUP

1 pound smoked
  sausage (sliced into
  1-inch pieces)
1 medium onion
  (chopped)
4 cups diced potatoes
1 teaspoon salt
1 teaspoon sweet basil
1/2 teaspoon pepper
1/4 teaspoon garlic
  powder
1 Tablespoon dried
  parsley
1 (15-1/2-ounce) can
  cream style corn
1 (15-1/2-ounce) can
  whole corn
1 (14-1/2-ounce) can
  beef broth
1 (14-1/2-ounce) can
  stewed tomatoes

Brown sausage and onion. Add remaining ingredients in order listed. Cover and simmer on low heat 45 minutes.

Natural was a necessity and not a fad in the Rural South. Herb "doctors" dispensed home remedies that promised a "cure" to the ill and ailing. Teas, soups, and poultices were brewed and contrived from every imaginable source that nature provided. In addition, every community had at least one person who was believed to have special powers for healing.

Miz Clem, a lady of considerable age, living in the piney woods of north-central Louisiana, was said to possess this power. She was very protective about her "gift," but on rare occasions she would parcel out tidbits of information. Once she revealed that "drawing fire" from a burn was her specialty. She also shared that "faith healing" must be passed on orally, nothing but one small chant could be written, and only those who believed could receive.

ALL-AMERICAN SOUP

1/2 pound lean ground beef

1 teaspoon paprika

1 teaspoon salt

1/4 teaspoon pepper

3 Tablespoons butter

3 Tablespoons all-purpose flour

3/4 cup shredded carrots

1/2 cup finely chopped onion

2 cloves garlic (minced)

1/4 teaspoon basil

1 teaspoon lemon juice

3 cups chicken broth

3 medium potatoes (cut into 1-inch cubes)

8 ounces process American cheese

1 cup milk

1 cup half & half

1 teaspoon dried parsley

Sprinkle paprika, salt, and pepper over meat. Brown meat in a heavy skillet. Drain and set aside.

Melt butter in a large, heavy pot. Stir in flour. Cook over medium heat 2-3 minutes. Add carrots, onion, garlic, basil, and lemon juice to hot mixture. Stir mixture until onions are tender (approximately 5 minutes). Add broth. Stir to blend. Add beef and potatoes. Cover and simmer until potatoes are tender (approximately 15 minutes). Add cheese and milk. Stir until cheese melts. Garnish with parsley.

"Home Remedy"
Boiled beet leaves brewed into a tea was used to treat a headache.

COUNTRY VEGETABLE SOUP

1 pound beef stew
1 (14-1/2-ounce) can
    stewed tomatoes
1 (15-ounce) can tomato
    sauce
6 cups water
4-1/2 cups frozen corn
2 cups sliced okra
2 cups diced potatoes
1 cup green beans
1-1/2 teaspoons salt
1 teaspoon pepper

In a large soup pot, combine beef stew, tomatoes, tomato sauce, and water. Bring to a rolling boil. Cover and reduce to medium heat. Cook 45 minutes, or until stew is tender.

Add remaining ingredients. Bring to a rolling boil. Cover and simmer 45 minutes.

Frozen vegetables are recommended for this recipe.

EASY CHICKEN NOODLE SOUP

6 chicken legs
4 cups water
2 chicken bouillon cubes
1-1/2 teaspoons salt
1/2 teaspoon pepper
1 Tablespoon butter
3 cups egg noodles

Combine water, bouillon cubes, salt, pepper, and butter in a 6-quart pot. Bring water to a boil. Add chicken and cook until tender. Using a slotted spoon, remove chicken from broth. Remove cooked chicken from bones. Bring broth to a rolling boil. Return chicken to liquid. Add noodles. Cover and simmer until noodles are tender.

Add more water if needed.

CORN AND TOMATO SOUP

6 cups frozen corn
1/2 pound beef stew
1 (14-1/2-ounce) can
   tomatoes
1 (15-ounce) can
   tomato sauce
2 cups beef broth
1 cup water
1/2 teaspoon salt
1/2 teaspoon pepper
3 medium potatoes
   (cubed)

Combine all ingredients, except potatoes, in a 3-quart pot. Heat until mixture reaches a rolling boil. Reduce heat and cover with a tight-fitting lid. Simmer over medium-low heat 20 minutes.

Add potatoes. Simmer 25 additional minutes or until meat is tender.

Add more water if needed.

"Home Remedy"
A home brew made from whiskey, honey, and lemon juice was a cold cure reserved just for Poppa.

REENA'S CORN AND POTATO SOUP

4 cups frozen corn

4 Tablespoons corn oil

3/4 cup chopped onion

1/4 cup chopped green pepper

1 clove garlic (minced)

1 (14-1/2-ounce) can chopped tomatoes

3 medium potatoes (cooked & diced)

1 small dried red pepper (crushed)

1 teaspoon salt

1/2 teaspoon pepper

1/4 teaspoon oregano

1/4 teaspoon cumin

3 cups chicken broth

2 cups half & half

Pour boiling water over corn. Let set 5 minutes. Drain corn thoroughly. Set aside.

Heat oil in a large soup pot. Sauté onion and green pepper until onion is clear. Add garlic and sauté 3 additional minutes. Add corn, tomatoes, potatoes, and seasonings. Bring mixture to a boil. Add chicken broth. Bring to a rolling boil. Simmer over low heat until potatoes are tender. Stir in half & half. Simmer 5 minutes.

HAM, BROCCOLI, AND CHEESE SOUP

1 (10-ounce] package frozen chopped broccoli (thawed)

1-1/2 cups water

3 teaspoons instant chicken bouillon granules

1 cup cooked & chopped ham

1 cup milk

1 cup half & half

1 cup shredded Swiss cheese

1/2 cup grated Cheddar cheese

1/2 teaspoon salt

1/8 teaspoon white pepper

1/8 teaspoon nutmeg

3 Tablespoons flour

In a large pot, bring water and bouillon granules to a rolling boil. Heat until granules have dissolved. Add broccoli, cover, and cook over medium heat 8-10 minutes. Stir in ham, milk, cheeses, seasonings, and nutmeg. Heat until cheese is melted.

Remove 1 cup soup mixture. In a small bowl, combine flour and liquid. Blend thoroughly. Return to soup mixture. Cook over low heat until mixture is thick and bubbly.

"Home Remedy"
Tallow, a firm white animal fat, was warmed slightly to make a poultice for chest colds.

CHUNKY POTATO SOUP

4 large potatoes (cut
  into 1-inch cubes)
1/2 cup butter
1/2 cup green onion
5 Tablespoons flour
1 quart milk
1 (14-1/2-ounce) can
  chicken broth
1 teaspoon salt
1/4 teaspoon pepper
1/4 teaspoon garlic
  powder
1/4 teaspoon sweet
  basil
1/2 pound bacon
  (cooked and
  crumbled)

Cover cubed potatoes with water. Cook until tender. Drain and set aside.

In a heavy pot, sauté green onion in butter. Stir in flour until well blended. Gradually pour milk and chicken broth over onion. Add seasonings and potatoes. Simmer until soup thickens (approximately 15-20 minutes).

Sprinkle bacon over soup before serving.

Additional milk may be added for desired consistency.

CREAM OF SQUASH SOUP

2 pounds yellow
   squash (sliced)
1 large onion (finely
   chopped)
1 clove garlic (minced)
1 (14-1/2-ounce) can
   chicken broth
4 Tablespoons butter
1 cup milk
1 cup half & half
1-1/2 teaspoons salt
1/2 teaspoon white
   pepper
3/4 teaspoon paprika

Cook squash, onion, and garlic in chicken broth 10-12 minutes over medium-high heat. Stir in butter. Allow mixture to cool thoroughly. Process mixture in a blender until creamy. Return to pot. Add milk, salt, and pepper. Whisk to blend. Cook over low heat until mixture is thoroughly heated.

Sprinkle with paprika before serving.

CREAM OF TURNIP SOUP

5 medium turnips
   (peeled & grated)
2 (14-1/2-ounce) cans
   chicken broth
3 Tablespoons butter
1/2 teaspoon sugar
1/2 teaspoon salt
1/8 teaspoon red
   pepper
1/2 cup milk
1/2 cup half & half
2 Tablespoons
   whipping cream
1/8 teaspoon nutmeg

Combine turnips, broth, butter, sugar, and seasonings in a heavy pot. Simmer over high heat until turnips are tender. Allow mixture to cool before spooning into a food processor or blender. Blend until smooth. Return to pot.

Stir in milk and cream. Heat thoroughly. Sprinkle with nutmeg just before serving.

Additional milk may be used for desired consistency.

CREAM OF TOMATO SOUP

**1 (14-1/2-ounce) can
whole tomatoes
1 (10-3/4-ounce) can
condensed tomato
soup
1 teaspoon sugar
1 Tablespoon butter
1/4 cup finely chopped
onion
1/4 cup finely chopped
celery
1/2 teaspoon salt
1/4 teaspoon pepper
1/4 teaspoon sweet
basil
1/4 teaspoon garlic
powder
1-1/2 cups half & half
1 cup chicken broth**

Pureé tomatoes in a blender. Add soup and sugar to tomatoes. Process to make a creamy mixture.

Sauté onion and celery in butter until tender. Add sauteéd vegetables to tomato mixture. Blend to purée. Pour soup into a heavy pot. Add seasonings.

Add half & half and broth to soup. Whisk to blend. Cover and simmer until thoroughly heated.

Additional liquid may be added for desired consistency.

HARVEST SOUP

1/2 pound smoked
   sausage (cut into
   1/4-inch slices)
2 cups apple cider
3 Tablespoons butter
2 small carrots
   (scraped & sliced)
1 (16-ounce) can
   pumpkin
1 (14-1/2-ounce) can
   chicken broth
1 teaspoon lemon juice
1/2 teaspoon cinnamon
1/8 teaspoon nutmeg
1/8 teaspoon salt
1/8 teaspoon white
   pepper
1-1/4 cups milk

Brown sausage. Drain and set aside.

Combine apple cider, butter, and carrots in a large saucepan. Cover and cook over medium heat 10 minutes or until carrots are tender.

Add pumpkin, broth, lemon juice, spices, and seasonings to mixture. Pour mixture into blender. Process until creamy. Return to pot. Add sausage and simmer 10 minutes. Add milk. Heat thoroughly.

"Home Remedy"
Poison ivy and okra stings were treated by applying a paste made from vinegar, buttermilk, baking soda, and salt.

CUCUMBER & TOMATO SALAD
(w/creamy or marinated dressing)

2 medium cucumbers
(peeled & thinly
sliced)

1 large tomato (cut into
small wedges)

1/2 purple onion
(sliced into rings)

3/4 teaspoon salt

1/4 teaspoon white
pepper

Combine prepared vegetables in a mixing bowl. Sprinkle with salt and pepper. Let set 20 minutes. Drain vegetables.

Either creamy or marinated dressing may be used on salad.

CREAMY DRESSING

3 Tablespoons sour
cream

1 Tablespoon
mayonnaise

2 Tablespoons apple
cider vinegar

1 Tablespoon sugar

I teaspoon lemon juice

1/4 teaspoon mustard

In a small mixing bowl, combine all ingredients. Whisk to blend. Pour over vegetables. Toss to mix. Chill several hours.

MARINATED DRESSING

1 cup white vinegar

3/4 cup sugar

1/4 cup olive oil

1/2 teaspoon cilantro

1/4 teaspoon salt

1/8 teaspoon red
pepper

Combine all ingredients. Heat thoroughly. Whisk to blend. Cool and pour over vegetables. Let set several hours.

TOSSED CORN AND HOMINY SALAD

1 (15-ounce) can white hominy (drained)

1 (15-ounce) can yellow corn (drained)

1/2 cup finely chopped purple onion

1 small green pepper (chopped)

1 small sweet red pepper (chopped)

1/4 cup olive oil

3 Tablespoons red wine vinegar

2 teaspoons sugar

1/2 teaspoon sweet basil

1/2 teaspoon salt

1/2 teaspoon black pepper

1 (8-ounce) package Colby cheese (cubed)

1/4 cup grated Parmesan cheese

Combine hominy and corn in colander. Rinse thoroughly. Lay vegetables on paper towel to blot until all excess moisture is removed. Toss vegetables, hominy, and corn in a large mixing bowl.

In a small mixing bowl combine oil, vinegar, and sugar. Whisk to blend. Add basil, salt, and pepper to liquid. Pour mixture over vegetables. Add cheese to mixture and toss. Refrigerate several hours.

"Home Remedy"
Tea made from boiling corn shucks was used to treat a variety of minor ailments.

SWEET AND SOUR CABBAGE SLAW

4 cups finely shredded cabbage

2 Tablespoons grated onion

1/2 teaspoon celery seed

2 Tablespoons sugar

2 Tablespoons apple cider vinegar

1/2 teaspoon salt

1/4 teaspoon white pepper

1/2 cup mayonnaise

Combine cabbage and onion.

In a separate bowl, combine remaining ingredients. Whisk to thoroughly blend. Pour dressing over cabbage. Toss. Refrigerate several hours before serving.

WILTED SALAD

8 slices bacon

1 head lettuce (torn into large pieces)

1 small onion (sliced into rings)

1/4 cup apple cider vinegar

1 Tablespoon sugar

1/4 teaspoon salt

1/4 teaspoon pepper

2 hard boiled eggs

Fry bacon until crisp. Drain and crumble. Save 1/4 cup bacon drippings.

In a large bowl, combine lettuce and onion. In a small saucepan, combine vinegar, bacon drippings, sugar, and seasonings. Bring to a rolling boil. Let cool 2-3 minutes. Pour over lettuce and onion rings. Toss lightly until greens are coated with dressing. Garnish with bacon and egg slices.

Spinach may be substituted for lettuce.

CARROT AND RAISIN SLAW

4 cups grated carrots
1 cup seedless raisins
1/2 cup chopped celery
1/2 cup sour cream
1 Tablespoon lemon
    juice
2 teaspoons sugar
1/2 teaspoon salt
1/2 teaspoon cinnamon
1/8 teaspoon cayenne
    pepper

Combine carrots, raisins, and celery.

In a separate bowl, combine remaining ingredients. Whisk to blend. Pour over carrot mixture. Toss to mix. Chill before serving.

CABBAGE AND APPLE SLAW

4 cups shredded
    cabbage
2 medium apples
    (cored & chopped)
1/2 cup salad dressing
4 Tablespoons lime
    juice
4 Tablespoons sugar
3/4 teaspoon salt
1/4 teaspoon pepper
1 cup chopped pecans
    (toasted)

Combine cabbage and apples (Apples should not be pared.)

Combine salad dressing, lime juice, sugar, and seasonings. Beat to blend. Spoon mixture over cabbage. Toss to mix. Fold in pecans. Chill thoroughly before serving.

POTATO SALAD

4 medium potatoes
2 teaspoons Creole
  seasoning
4 boiled eggs (finely
  chopped)
5 Tablespoons
  mayonnaise
2 Tablespoons sweet
  pickle relish
1 Tablespoon mustard
1/2 teaspoon sugar
1 teaspoon salt
1/2 teaspoon onion
  powder
1/2 teaspoon garlic
  powder
1/4 teaspoon pepper
1/8 teaspoon red
  pepper

Quarter and leave potatoes in skins. Cover with water. Add Creole seasoning to water. Boil until tender. Drain and remove skins. Set aside to cool before cutting into 1/2-inch cubes.

In a separate bowl, combine remaining ingredients. Mix thoroughly. Add mixture to potatoes. Toss lightly to mix.

MARINATED RICE SALAD

1 cup instant rice
1/2 cup Italian salad
   dressing
1/2 cup water
1 cup tiny English peas
1/2 cup chopped
   pimiento
3/4 cup sliced mush-
   rooms
1 small onion
   (chopped)
1 stalk celery (chopped)
1 cup mayonnaise
1 cup chopped walnuts

Combine salad dressing and water. Cook rice in mixture according to package directions.

Drain peas, pimiento, and mushrooms. Combine with onion and celery. Add rice to vegetables. Fold in mayonnaise and walnuts. Refrigerator overnight.

"SWEET PEA" SALAD

1 (15-1/2-ounce) can
   English peas
1/3 cup finely chopped
   onion
1 Tablespoon sweet
   pickle relish
3 hard boiled eggs
   (finely chopped)
1/4 teaspoon salt
1/4 teaspoon pepper
1/3 cup mayonnaise
2/3 cup grated Cheddar
   cheese

Drain peas. Combine with remaining ingredients.

Additional mayonnaise may be added.

LOUISIANA SHRIMP SLAW

1 pound cooked
   shrimp
3 cups shredded red
   cabbage
3 cups shredded green
   cabbage
1/2 cup grated carrots
1/4 cup chopped
   parsley

Combine ingredients.

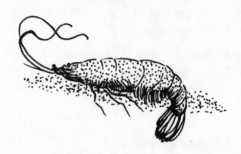

DRESSING

1 cup salad dressing
1 cup buttermilk
1 (16-ounce) package
   original Ranch
   Hidden Valley
   dressing mix
1/4 teaspoon Creole
   seasoning
1/4 teaspoon sweet
   basil

Combine all ingredients. Whisk to blend. Pour over slaw. Toss to mix. Chill 2-3 hours before serving.

BAYOU SALAD

1 cup rice
2 cups chicken broth
1 (16-ounce) package
  crawfish tails
1 teaspoon paprika
1/4 cup margarine
1-1/4 cups chopped
  celery
3/4 cup frozen green peas
  (thawed)
3 Tablespoons finely
  chopped pimientos
3/4 cup salad dressing
1 Tablespoon lemon juice
3/4 teaspoon salt
1/4 teaspoon pepper
1 small head lettuce
  (shredded)

In a medium-size saucepan, bring broth to a rolling boil. Add rice. Stir and cover. Reduce heat to a low simmer. Cook 20 minutes. Let cool.

Sprinkle crawfish tails with paprika. Cook crawfish in melted margarine. Remove from skillet and drain excess liquid.

Combine vegetables, salad dressing, lemon juice, salt, and pepper. Add crawfish and rice. Toss lightly. Chill thoroughly.

Serve on a bed of lettuce.

DELUXE TUNA SALAD

1 (6-1/2 ounce) can white
  tuna (packed in spring
  water)
3 hard boiled eggs (finely
  chopped)
3 Tablespoons salad
  dressing
2 teaspoons mustard
2 teaspoons sweet pickle
  relish
1/2 teaspoon sugar
1/2 teaspoon salt
1/2 teaspoon pepper

Drain tuna thoroughly. Combine tuna and eggs. Add remaining ingredients to tuna mixture. Stir to mix well. Use an electric mixer to blend all ingredients. (This step is very important.)

Excellent for sandwiches or spreads.

MACARONI AND HAM SALAD

3 cups cooked macaroni
1 Tablespoon butter
(melted)
2 cups cooked ham (cut
into 1-inch cubes)
2 cups cubed Cheddar
cheese
2 hard-boiled eggs
(finely grated)
1 cup finely chopped
celery
1/2 cup finely chopped
onion
1/3 cup sweet pickle
relish
1 cup Ranch-style
dressing
2 teaspoons mustard
1/4 teaspoon salt
1/4 teaspoon pepper

Pour melted butter over hot
macaroni. Add ham.

Combine remaining ingredients
in the order listed. Toss to mix
thoroughly. Chill 12 hours.

"Home Remedy"
*Tea made from the root of a sassafras
tree dug in spring was used for "build-
ing blood" of the sickly.*

PASTA SALAD

1 (7-ounce) package small macaroni

2 (6-ounce) cans chicken breast

2 (11-ounce) cans mandarin oranges (drained)

1 large apple (chopped)

1/2 cup finely chopped celery

1 cup salad dressing

1 Tablespoon sugar

2 Tablespoons fresh squeezed lemon juice

2 Tablespoons whipping cream

1/2 cup toasted pecans

Cook pasta according to package directions. Rinse with cold water. Drain and set aside.

Combine chicken, oranges, apple, and celery.

In a small bowl, combine remaining ingredients, except pecans. Whisk to blend. Pour over pasta and toss to mix. Fold in chicken mixture. Cover and chill 2-3 hours. Sprinkle with pecans.

Serve on a bed of shredded lettuce.

"Home Remedy"
An old "rag" was tied snugly around an aching head to relieve the pain.

STRAWBERRY SALAD

1 cup chopped pecans
1/2 cup sugar
1 teaspoon butter
8-9 cups mixed salad
  greens
1-1/2 cups sliced
  strawberries

Melt butter in a small skillet. Add pecans and sugar to butter. Cook over medium heat 6-8 minutes or until sugar is melted. Stir mixture frequently. Remove nuts from skillet to wax paper. Cool. Break into pieces.

Toss salad greens and strawberries. Sprinkle with pecans.

DRESSING
3/4 cup olive oil
2/3 cup apple cider
  vinegar
2/3 cup sugar
1 teaspoon salt
1/2 teaspoon black
  pepper
1/8 teaspoon red
  pepper
1 Tablespoon dried
  parsley

Combine ingredients in order listed. Heat over medium heat 4 minutes or until sugar is dissolved. Cool 10 minutes. Pour dressing into a jar and shake vigorously. Pour over salad before serving.

"Home Remedy"
Congestion was treated by eating a tablespoon of honey six times a day.

FRESH FRUIT SALAD

1 pint strawberries
(sliced)
1 medium apple
(unpeeled, cored
& chopped)
1 medium pear
(unpeeled, cored
& chopped)
1 medium peach
(peeled
& chopped)
1 medium orange
(peeled &
chopped)
1 cup blueberries

Layer fruit in large glass bowl in order listed above.

DRESSING
1 cup fresh squeezed
orange juice
1/4 cup lemon juice
3/4 cup sugar
1 teaspoon orange
peel
1/2 teaspoon
cinnamon
1/4 teaspoon almond
extract
2 teaspoons corn-
starch

In a small saucepan, heat juices, sugar, orange peel, cinnamon, and almond extract until liquid boils. Remove 1/3 cup of hot mixture and stir in cornstarch. Return mixture to saucepan. Heat, stirring constantly, until mixture becomes slightly thickened. Let cool thoroughly. Pour over layered fruit. Cover and chill several hours. Toss salad before serving.

TUTTI-FRUTTI DESSERT SALAD

1 (17-ounce) can fruit
    cocktail (with liquid)
1 (8-1/4-ounce) can
    pineapple chunks
    (with liquid)
1 (11-ounce) can
    mandarin oranges
    (with liquid)
1/2 cup shredded coconut
2 Tablespoons lemon
    juice
1 (3-3/4-ounce) package
    instant lemon pudding
    mix
2 bananas (thinly sliced)
1 (8-ounce) carton pre-
    pared frozen topping

Combine fruit and lemon juice. Toss to mix. Sprinkle dry pudding mix over fruit. Chill several hours.

Stir bananas and frozen topping into fruit mixture.

FROZEN FRUIT DESSERT SALAD

1 (8-ounce) package
    cream cheese
    (softened)
1 (8-ounce) carton frozen
    whipped topping
    (thawed)
1 (21-ounce) can
    strawberry pie filling
1 (11-ounce) can
    mandarin oranges
    (drained)
1 (8-ounce) can pineapple
    bits (drained)

Combine cream cheese and whipped topping. Blend thoroughly. Gradually add fruit filling. Fold in oranges and pineapple. Line bottom of a 9x5x3-inch loaf pan with wax paper. Pour fruit mixture into pan. Freeze overnight. Let stand at room temperature for 10 minutes before serving. Cut into thin slices.

APPLE AND PEAR SALAD

1 apple
1 pear
1 Tablespoon lemon
   juice
1 (11-ounce) can
   mandarin oranges
   (drained)
1 (17-ounce) can fruit
   cocktail (drained)
1 (8-ounce) carton
   frozen whipped
   topping (thawed)
3/4 teaspoon cream of
   tartar
1 cup chopped pecans

Pare, core, and chop apple and pear. Squeeze lemon juice over fruit. Let set several minutes. Combine all fruits. Use paper towel to remove any excess liquid from canned and fresh fruit. Chill 15 minutes in freezer.

Sprinkle cream of tartar over topping. Stir lightly to mix. Fold topping and pecans into chilled fruit. Chill at least 30 minutes before serving.

"Home Remedy"
Fresh berry juice was used to treat stomach disorders.

GRAMMY'S AMBROSIA

1 (8-ounce) package cream cheese (softened)

1/2 (14-ounce) can condensed milk

2 (17-ounce) cans fruit cocktail (drained)

1 (8-ounce) can pineapple tidbits (drained)

2 (6-ounce) jars cherries (drained & cut in halves)

3/4 cup chopped pecans (toasted)

Combine cream cheese and condensed milk. Whip to make a creamy mixture. Pour mixture over drained fruit and pecans. Refrigerate several hours.

Excellent over pound cake or spice cake.

CRANBERRY RELISH

3/4 pound tart apples
1/2 pound oranges
1/4 pound cranberries
1 cup sugar

Core apples. Peel and remove seeds from oranges. Grind all fruits together. Add sugar and cover tightly. Chill at least 24 hours before serving.

vegetables

*M*onday came only once a week, thank goodness, because Monday was wash day. Summer wasn't so bad, but, during winter, wash day was pure misery. The task at hand began with an early search for wood. Then came the cutting and dragging and hauling the kindling back to the house. Mama would sort and pile the clothes while water was "drawn" from the well. Exactly thirteen buckets were needed to fill that old wash pot. The black pot, pitted and burned from hundreds of wash days, gave up a misty steam as the fire roared and crackled around it. Two rusty, old tubs, on a hand-hewn wash bench, were filled for washing and rinsing. As the white clothes boiled slowly in that old black wash pot, Mama picked up the batten stick, worn smooth from stirring, and wielded a hand to keep the boiling clothes stirred and covered. A rub-board, worn from knuckles working up and down the ridges, was used to remove the soil.

After a time, Mama poured a magic potion from a dark blue bottle into the rinse water. When the water and bluing met, a spidery maze cut through the clean cool liquid. Garments were 'wrung' and dumped into the rinse water that was, now, sky blue in color. The clothes line pole was lowered so that the line was within tip-toe reach. 'Wrung dry' clothes were hung and attached with wooden pins taken from a hanging cloth bag.

The fire was rekindled and the ordeal repeated with colored clothes. By late afternoon, all the fresh-washed clothes that had been hung in an orderly fashion were dry and ready to bring in, sort, fold, and prepare for ironing day - usually Tuesday.

vegetables

smothered potatoes, green beans, and sausage, *94*

border beans and rice, *95*

saucy pork and beans, *96*

lima beans and sausage / baked lima beans, *97*

green bean puff / garlic green beans, *98*

harvard beets, *99*

broccoli and cheese, *100*

baked cauliflower/ t-bo's cabbage, *101*

sunshine carrots, *102*

corn casserole, *103*

cream-style corn / pan-fried mexican corn, *104*

corn salsa, *105*

auntie's purple hull peas, *106*

hoppin' john, *107*

pan-fried onion rings / fried onion rings, *108*

potatoes casey, *109*

creamy mashed potatoes /country fried potato logs, *110*

stuffed potatoes / baked potato w/sauce, *111*

sweet potato logs, *112*

candied sweet potatoes, *113*

baked squash casserole, *114*

mamma starnes' squash dish, *115*

vegetable skillet / skillet okra and tomatoes, *116*

SMOTHERED POTATOES, GREEN BEANS, AND SAUSAGE

1/2 pound smoked link sausage
1/2 cup coarsely chopped onion
1 Tablespoon butter
4 medium potatoes (cubed)
1/2 cup water
1 (16-ounce) package frozen green beans
1/2 teaspoon salt
1/4 teaspoon pepper

Slice sausage diagonally into 1/2-inch pieces.

Sauté onion in butter 2 minutes. Add sausage to onion. Cook over medium heat 5 minutes or until sausage begins to brown. Add potatoes and 1/2 cup water (or enough to cover bottom of pot). Cover and simmer until potatoes are partially cooked. Add green beans. Cover and simmer until beans are tender. Turn sausage and vegetables at least twice while cooking.

In earlier times, the land was the important link to survival. Every community had at least one person who was believed to have the most wisdom about nature in relationship to the most productive planting time. In an area outside Natchez, Mississippi, Miz Sophie held this distinction. She knew best about when to plant, what to plant, and how to plant. Miz Sophie even brought her own mule to help prepare gardens for a bountiful harvest.

BORDER BEANS

1 (16-ounce) package dried pinto beans

2 quarts water

1 (14-ounce) can whole tomatoes

1 (1.25-ounce) package taco seasoning mix

1 (4.5-ounce) can chopped green chilies

1 cup finely chopped onion

3 cloves garlic (minced)

2 teaspoons salt

1 teaspoon cumin

1/2 teaspoon red pepper

Cover beans with water. Bring to a boil in Dutch oven. Reduce heat to simmer. Cook 2-1/2 hours or until beans are tender.

Add remaining ingredients. Leave uncovered while cooking. Simmer 1-1/2 hours. Additional water may be added as needed for desired consistency.

Serve over rice.

SAUCY PORK AND BEANS

1 pound ground
   sausage
2 (16-ounce) cans pork
   and beans
1/2 cup grated Cheddar
   cheese
2/3 cup finely chopped
   onion
1/4 cup brown sugar
1/3 cup barbecue sauce
2 Tablespoons
   molasses
2 Tablespoons
   Worcestershire
   sauce
1 Tablespoon white
   vinegar
1 Tablespoon chili
   powder
1/4 teaspoon salt
1/4 teaspoon pepper
1/4 teaspoon garlic
   powder
1/4 teaspoon liquid
   smoke

Brown sausage. Blot with paper towel to remove excess grease. Combine sausage and remaining ingredients. Mix thoroughly.

Bake at 350 degrees - 1 hour.

The South begins and ends with the land. Whether rich delta topsoil or piney woods loam or somewhere in between, a Southerner's pride lies in his roots that are deeply embedded beneath the warm, moist soil.

LIMA BEANS AND SAUSAGE

1 (1-pound) package dried lima beans
2 quarts water
1 teaspoon sugar
1/2 teaspoon salt
1/4 teaspoon pepper
1/2 large onion
3 bay leaves
1 pound link sausage (sliced into 1/4-inch wafers)

In a 5-quart pot, bring water to a rolling boil. Add beans, sugar, salt, pepper, onion, and bay leaves. Cover and cook 1 hour over medium heat.

Add sausage. Simmer 1 hour or until beans are tender. (Liquid in beans will thicken the longer cooked.) Remove onion half and bay leaves before serving.

BAKED LIMA BEANS

1 (1-pound) package dried lima beans
8 slices bacon
3/4 cup chopped onion
1 clove garlic (minced)
2 (8-ounce) cans tomato sauce
1/4 cup firmly packed brown sugar
2 teaspoons mustard
3/4 teaspoon salt
1/2 teaspoon oregano
1/2 teaspoon sweet basil
1/4 teaspoon pepper

Cover beans with water. Bring to a rolling boil. Cover and cook over medium heat until beans are barely tender. Drain beans, reserving 1/2 cup liquid.

Sauté bacon, onion, and garlic until bacon is browned. Drain excess grease from bacon. In a large mixing bowl, combine bacon, beans, and remaining ingredients. Add 1/2 cup reserved liquid from beans. Pour into a greased 2-1/2-quart baking dish. Cover.

Bake at 350 degrees - 40-50 minutes.

GREEN BEAN PUFF

2 (10-ounce) packages
  frozen French-style
  green beans
1/4 cup finely chopped
  onion
1/2 cup salad dressing
1 teaspoon mustard
1 teaspoon vinegar
1/2 teaspoon sugar
1/2 teaspoon salt
1/4 teaspoon pepper
4 Tablespoons milk
1 egg white (stiffly
  beaten)
1/4 teaspoon paprika

Steam green beans and onion until beans are tender. Layer vegetables in a greased casserole dish.

Combine salad dressing, mustard, vinegar, sugar, seasonings, and milk. Blend thoroughly. Fold beaten egg white into mixture. Pile mixture over beans. Sprinkle with paprika.

Bake at 375 degrees - 20 minutes or until top is browned.

GARLIC GREEN BEANS

1 (16-ounce) package
  frozen green beans
2 Tablespoons olive oil
1/4 cup finely chopped
  onion
2 cloves garlic (minced)
1/2 cup cooked &
  cubed ham
1 Tablespoon red wine
  vinegar
2 teaspoons sugar
1 teaspoon salt
1/4 teaspoon white
  pepper

Thaw and drain green beans.

Heat oil in a heavy skillet. Add onion, garlic, and ham to oil. Sauté until vegetables are soft. Add vinegar, sugar, and seasonings. Heat thoroughly. Stir in beans. Cover and simmer over medium heat 15-20 minutes.

HARVARD BEETS

1 (15-ounce) can
   sliced beets
1/4 teaspoon salt
2 Tablespoons sugar
2 teaspoons
   cornstarch
2 Tablespoons
   vinegar
1 Tablespoon butter

Drain beets and reserve liquid. In a medium saucepan, combine salt, sugar, and cornstarch. Add reserved liquid from beets. Cook over medium heat. Stir constantly until mixture thickens. Add vinegar, butter, and beets. Heat thoroughly.

BROCCOLI AND CHEESE

1 (16-ounce) package frozen chopped broccoli

3/4 cup finely chopped onion

1 clove garlic (minced)

2 Tablespoons butter

1 (8-ounce) jar process cheese spread

1 (10-3/4-ounce) can cream of mushroom soup

1 (5-ounce) can evaporated milk

3 cups cooked rice

Thaw, drain, and blot dry broccoli.

Sauté onion and garlic in butter until tender. Add broccoli to onion. Cook 5 minutes, stirring constantly. Remove from heat. Stir in cheese spread, mushroom soup, and milk. Add rice and blend thoroughly. Pour mixture into a large baking dish.

Bake at 325 degrees - 30 minutes or until bubbly.

BAKED CAULIFLOWER
(w/cheese sauce)

1 medium head cauli-
flower (broken into
small pieces)

Cover cauliflower with water. Cook until tender. Drain thoroughly.

SAUCE
2 Tablespoons butter
1 Tablespoon corn-
starch
1 cup milk
1/2 teaspoon salt
1/4 teaspoon white
pepper
1/4 teaspoon mustard
1 cup grated Cheddar
cheese
1/2 cup shredded
Swiss cheese

In a small saucepan, melt butter. Stir in cornstarch. Slowly add milk, stirring constantly. Add salt, pepper, and mustard. Continue stirring over medium heat until mixture thickens. Remove from heat. Stir in cheeses. Heat until cheeses are melted. Pour over steamed cauliflower.

T-BO'S CABBAGE

1 medium head
cabbage
2 slices bacon (cut
into 2-inch strips)
1 teaspoon salt
1/2 teaspoon pepper
1 apple (cored &
sliced)

Core and cut cabbage into large wedge shaped pieces. Separate leaves. Soak in ice water 15 minutes. Drain thoroughly.

In a heavy pot, sear bacon 1-2 minutes. Add cabbage, salt, pepper, and apple pieces to pot. (Do not add water.) Cover and cook over medium heat 15 minutes. Cabbage will be slightly crunchy. (Cook longer if more tender cabbage is desired.)

SUNSHINE CARROTS

2-1/2 pounds carrots (thinly sliced)

2 Tablespoons corn-starch

1/2 cup water

1-1/2 cups orange juice

1/4 cup sugar

1 teaspoon lemon juice

1 teaspoon ginger

1/8 teaspoon cinnamon

Cover carrots with water. Bring to a rolling boil. Cook over medium heat 5 minutes. Cover and simmer over low heat 6 minutes. (Do not overcook so that carrots will remain slightly crunchy.) Drain carrots and set aside.

In a small saucepan, combine cornstarch and water. Mix well. Stir in orange juice, sugar, and lemon juice until mixture is blended thoroughly. Add ginger and cinnamon. Cook over medium-low heat until mixture thickens. Add drained carrots to saucepan. Heat thoroughly.

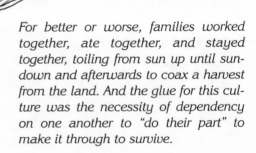

For better or worse, families worked together, ate together, and stayed together, toiling from sun up until sundown and afterwards to coax a harvest from the land. And the glue for this culture was the necessity of dependency on one another to "do their part" to make it through to survive.

CORN CASSEROLE

1 pound ground beef
1/4 cup butter
1 medium onion (finely
   chopped)
2 (15-ounce) cans
   cream-style corn
1/2 cup water
2 eggs (beaten)
2 cups grated Cheddar
   cheese
1 (8-1/2-ounce) box jiffy
   cornbread mix
1/2 teaspoon Creole
   seasoning
1/2 teaspoon salt
1/2 teaspoon pepper

Brown meat and drain excess grease.

Sauté onion in butter. Combine remaining ingredients in order listed. Add browned beef and mix well. Pour mixture into a greased 13x9x2-inch baking dish.

Bake at 350 degrees - 45 minutes.

CREAM-STYLE CORN

4 cups frozen corn
1/3 cup butter
2 Tablespoons sugar
1/2 cup half & half
1/2 teaspoon salt
1/4 teaspoon white
    pepper

In a large skillet, melt butter. Add corn. Cook over medium heat 5 minutes. Add sugar, half-&-half, and seasonings. Simmer approximately 10 minutes or until excess liquid has been absorbed.

PAN-FRIED MEXICAN CORN

2 (11-ounce) cans
    Mexican corn
3 Tablespoons butter
3 Tablespoons finely
    chopped onion
3 Tablespoons finely
    chopped green
    pepper
1/4 cup chicken
    broth
1/2 teaspoon salt
1/4 teaspoon pepper
1/4 teaspoon sweet
    basil

Drain liquid from corn. Melt butter in skillet. Sauté onion and pepper 3-4 minutes. Add corn, chicken broth, and seasonings. Simmer 10 minutes or until liquid is absorbed. Stir frequently to prevent sticking.

CORN SALSA

3 (11-ounce) cans Mexican
   corn (drained)
1 (4-ounce) can chopped
   green chilies (drained)
1 (2-1/2-ounce) can sliced
   black olives
2 medium tomatoes
   (chopped)
3 Tablespoons chopped
   jalapeno peppers
3 Tablespoons white vine-
   gar
1 Tablespoon sugar
1/3 cup olive oil
1 teaspoon cilantro
1/4 teaspoon garlic powder
1/4 teaspoon salt

Combine all ingredients in a
large glass bowl. Mix well.
Cover and let set overnight.

AUNTIE'S PURPLE HULL PEAS

1 (16-ounce) package
frozen purple hull
peas
3 cups water
1 Tablespoon chili
powder
1 teaspoon Creole
seasoning
1 teaspoon sugar
1 (16-ounce) package
ground hot
sausage
1 (14-1/2-ounce) can
stewed tomatoes

In a large heavy pot, cover peas with water. Add chili powder, Creole seasoning, and sugar. Cover and cook over medium heat 30 minutes or until peas are tender. Stir occasionally. Add additional water as needed.

Brown and drain sausage. Add to peas. Stir in tomatoes. Cover and cook over medium heat an additional 20 minutes.

For more "zip", substitute a can of Cajun Recipe Stewed Tomatoes.

Now 71 years of age, Big Baby shares this story, "Coming from a family of nine children during the Depression was not an easy time to grow up. We all had to work. The older children picked dried peas for 1 cent a pound to buy school clothes. Mama made our clothes from material that cost 15 cents a yard. And we were happy to be able to earn the money."

HOPPIN' JOHN

2-1/2 cups dried
  black-eyed peas
1 quart water
1 pound ham
  (chopped)
3/4 cup finely chopped
  onion
1/2 cup finely chopped
  green onion
2 Tablespoons
  chopped jalapeño
  peppers
1/4 cup chopped
  green pepper
2 teaspoons Creole
  seasoning
2 cups hot cooked rice

Cover peas with water in a large saucepan. Bring mixture to a rolling boil. Cook over high heat 5 minutes. Remove from heat. Let set 1-1/2 - 2 hours. Drain thoroughly.

In a heavy pot, bring 1 quart water to a rolling boil. Add ham and cook over high heat 15 minutes. Add drained peas. Cover and simmer 30 minutes. Add onions, peppers, and seasoning. Cover and simmer until peas are tender (approximately 25 minutes). Stir hot rice into mixture.

PAN FRIED ONION

4 large white onions
3 Tablespoons butter
3 Tablespoons apple
   cider vinegar
3 Tablespoons brown
   sugar
2 teaspoons granu-
   lated sugar
1/4 teaspoon Creole
   seasoning
1/4 teaspoon paprika

Peel and slice onions into thin rings.

Melt butter in skillet. Add onions to hot butter for 2-3 minutes or long enough to coat rings. Pour vinegar over onions. Add remaining ingredients. Cook over medium heat 5-6 minutes or until onions are tender but still crispy.

FRIED ONION RINGS

1-1/2 cups flour
1-1/2 cups beer
3 large onions
   (peeled & sliced
   into rings)

Mix flour and beer to make a thick batter. Cover and let set at room temperature for 3 hours. Dip onion rings in batter. Deep fry in hot oil until golden brown.

POTATOES CASEY

6 medium potatoes
 (peeled & cut into
 1/4-inch rounds)
1/2 teaspoon salt
1/4 teaspoon pepper
1/8 teaspoon garlic
 powder
1 pound link sausage
 (cut into 1/4-inch
 wafers)
1 Tablespoon butter
1 medium onion
 (finely chopped)
1 medium bell pepper
 (finely chopped)
12 ounces Cheddar
 cheese (shredded)

Cover potatoes with water and boil until tender (Do not over-cook.) Lift potatoes with a slotted spoon from water to prevent breakage. Drain. Sprinkle with seasonings.

Cover sausage with water and boil 10 minutes. Drain and blot with paper towel.

Sauté onion and bell pepper in butter until tender. (Do not brown vegetables.) In a greased 2-quart oblong casserole dish, layer potatoes, sausage, sautéed vegetables, and cheese. Repeat with remaining ingredients. Cover to bake.

Bake at 325 degrees 15 minutes or until cheese is bubbly.

Grandpa Noah was born in 1865. His wife's family had home-steaded a tract of Louisiana piney woods land. He "raised" sixteen children as a dirt farmer on this land. He always main-tained that a man is never poor if he has a piece of ground to call his own. Two of his sons later bought the surrounding property for 50 cents an acre in the 1920's. This land is still held by family members.

CREAMY MASHED POTATOES

5 large potatoes
3/4 teaspoon salt
4 Tablespoons butter
3/4 cup hot milk
2 egg yolks
1/4 teaspoon garlic
    powder
1/8 teaspoon black
    pepper
3/4 cup grated
    Mozzarella cheese
1/4 cup grated
    Parmesan cheese
2 Tablespoons dried
    parsley

Peel potatoes and cut into 1-inch cubes. Cover with water. Add salt. Cover and boil over high heat until potatoes are tender. (Approximately 25 minutes.) Drain thoroughly.

Add butter to potatoes. Mash thoroughly. Add hot milk, and egg yolks. Whip with electric mixer. Add seasonings. Stir in cheeses. Pour mixture into a greased 2-quart baking dish. Sprinkle with parsley.

Bake at 350 degrees - 15 minutes. Broil an additional 10 minutes or until potatoes are browned and crusty.

COUNTRY FRIED POTATO LOGS

4 medium potatoes
2 teaspoons salt
1 teaspoon pepper
1 teaspoon paprika
1 cup flour

Slice potatoes lengthwise into 1/2-inch strips. (Potatoes may be peeled or left in skins.) Combine 1 teaspoon salt, 1/2 teaspoon pepper, and 1/2 teaspoon paprika. Mix well. Sprinkle over potatoes. Let set 5-10 minutes.

Combine remaining salt, pepper, paprika, and flour in a brown bag. Close top and shake to mix. Drop a few potato logs at a time into bag. Shake vigorously to coat. Drop potatoes in hot oil. Fry until lightly browned.

STUFFED POTATOES

6 pounds large baking
potatoes
1 (8-ounce) package
cream cheese
1 (16-ounce) carton
sour cream
1/4 cup finely
chopped green
onion
1 teaspoon Creole
seasoning
1 teaspoon salt
1/4 teaspoon pepper
1/4 cup bacon bits
1 cup grated Cheddar
cheese

Wrap potatoes in foil. Bake until soft. Remove from oven. Do not remove foil. Slice potatoes in half lengthwise. Scoop out inside of each potato. Combine potato pulp with all remaining ingredients, except cheese. Mix well, but do not mash. Spoon mixture back into potato skins. Sprinkle each stuffed potato with cheese. Arrange on baking sheet.

Bake at 325 degrees - 20 minutes or until mixture is thoroughly heated.

BAKED POTATOES WITH SAUCE

6 medium baked
potatoes
1 (16-ounce) carton
sour cream
1 (8-ounce) jar
English cheese
spread
1 teaspoon grated
onion
12 slices cooked
bacon (crumbled)

Combine sour cream, cheese, and onion. Beat to mix. Pour over hot baked potato. Sprinkle crumbled bacon over potato.

Red potatoes may also be used for baking. These potatoes have more flavor.

SWEET POTATO LOGS

4 medium sweet
   potatoes (baked
   in skins)
1 teaspoon vanilla
   extract
1 cup sugar
1 egg
1/4 cup milk
3 Tablespoons flour
1-1/2 teaspoons
   cinnamon
1 cup chopped
   pecans
1/2 cup raisins
4 Tablespoons
   melted butter
3 cups shredded
   coconut

Peel and mash sweet potatoes. Combine sweet potatoes with all ingredients, except butter and coconut. Mix well. Shape into 8 potato logs.

Drizzle melted butter over logs. Roll in coconut.

May be frozen.

CANDIED SWEET POTATOES

4 medium sweet
   potatoes
1/4 cup butter
3 cups sugar
1 teaspoon vanilla
   extract

Peel and slice potatoes into 1/2-inch round slices. In a large skillet, cover potatoes with water. Add butter and cook over medium heat until potatoes are barely tender. Carefully remove potatoes from liquid (reserving liquid). Layer sweet potatoes in a large cast-iron pot.

In a medium saucepan, add sugar to liquid where potatoes were cooked. Bring to a rolling boil. Cook until liquid thickens and a thread forms when spoon is lifted out of mixture. Add extract. Beat to mix. Pour syrup over potatoes.

Bake at 300 degrees - 25 minutes.

BAKED SQUASH CASSEROLE

2 pounds squash
  (sliced)
1 small onion
  (chopped)
1/3 cup finely chopped
  green pepper
1 teaspoon chopped
  jalapeño pepper
3/4 cup mayonnaise
2 eggs (beaten)
1/2 cup grated
  Cheddar cheese
1/2 cup grated
  Parmesan cheese
1/2 teaspoon salt
1/4 teaspoon cayenne
  pepper
1/2 cup herb-seasoned
  stuffing mix
3 Tablespoons
  margarine (melted)

Steam squash, onion, and peppers until tender.

Combine mayonnaise and eggs. Beat to blend. Stir in cheeses, salt, and pepper. Add vegetables and mix well. Spoon into a greased casserole dish.

Combine stuffing mix and margarine to make a crumbly mixture. Sprinkle over squash.

Bake at 325 degrees - 25-30 minutes.

MAMMA STARNES' SQUASH DISH

2 pounds squash
(peeled & sliced)
1 medium onion
(finely chopped)
1 teaspoon salt
1/4 teaspoon pepper
2 teaspoons sugar
1 egg (beaten)
1 can (10-3/4-ounce)
cheese soup
1-1/4 cups grated
Cheddar cheese
3/4 cup yellow corn-
meal
1/4 cup margarine
1/4 cup bread crumbs

Barely cover squash and onion with water. Season with salt and pepper. Cook until tender. Drain.

In a separate bowl, combine sugar, egg, cheese soup, 1 cup Cheddar cheese, and cornmeal. Beat to mix. Melt margarine in baking dish. Spoon squash mixture into a buttered dish. Pour cheese mixture over squash. Combine remaining 1/4 cup Cheddar cheese and bread-crumbs. Sprinkle over squash.

Bake at 350 degrees - 30 minutes.

Mamma's work was never ending. She was up first and to bed last. Seldom complaining, she trudged through her daily tasks softly humming about the "sweet by and by."

vegetables

VEGETABLE SKILLET

3 Tablespoons butter
1 Tablespoon
  vegetable oil
4 small zucchini (thinly
  sliced)
1 cup finely chopped
  onion
1 small green pepper
  (finely chopped)
2 cups chopped
  tomatoes
1-1/2 cups frozen corn
1 teaspoon salt
1 teaspoon oregano
1/2 teaspoon sweet
  basil
1/2 teaspoon pepper

Heat butter and oil in a large skillet. Sauté zucchini, onion, and green pepper 5 minutes. Add tomatoes, corn, and seasonings. Simmer 20-25 minutes. Stir frequently.

SKILLET OKRA AND TOMATOES

2 Tablespoons olive oil
1 cup chopped onion
2 cloves garlic
  (minced)
1 (14-1/2-ounce) can
  diced tomatoes
4 cups sliced okra
1 (.67-ounce) package
  Italian seasoning
1/2 teaspoon salt
1/4 teaspoon pepper

Sauté onion and garlic in olive oil until tender. Add tomatoes, okra, Italian seasoning, salt, and pepper to sauteéd vegetables. Simmer 12 minutes, stirring occasionally. Cover and simmer additional 20 minutes.

poultry

*E*lusive shadows danced across the window as a gentle breeze silently stirred the sprouts of new leaves. Golden rays of a new moon spread over the darkness, softening the blackness of a spring night. Perched high and nestled among branches in the old Chinaberry tree, a lone mocking bird chirped out messages that a new season had arrived.

As spring faded into summer, it was time to dig out the pea shooter made from a section of Grandpa's broken fishing cane. An abundance of hanging berries promised to provide ammunition enough to renew challenges of previous years. Mock wars were daily occurrences when Chinaberries were "in season." Mama's chickens were preferred targets, but no one ventured around corners of the house without a quick peep in anticipation of a possible ambush. In the blistering heat of long, hot days of summer, the once-hard green berries were rendered useless for backyard shoot-outs, but all was not lost. The remaining berries, fermented by the hot sun of summer, became an intoxicating delicacy to the mocking bird and her new family.

Then, as nature continued her endless task, the leaves on the old tree fell, and a layer of mushy yellow berries covered the ground. Once again, the pea shooter was retired to the bottom drawer of the "chiff robe" until next year.

poultry

smothered chicken and gravy, **120**

easy baked chicken and gravy, **121**

spicy southern fried chicken, **122**

oven fried chicken, **123**

garlic baked chicken, **124**

oven-barbecued chicken / easy baked chicken loaf, **125**

stuffed chicken breast with crab sauce, **126**

dish pan chicken and cornbread dressing, **127**

chicken and cornbread casserole, **128**

mozzarella chicken with red sauce, **129**

chicken noodle casserole, **130**

overnight chicken casserole, **131**

chicken vegetable skillet / chicken and wild rice dish, **132**

chicken asparagus casserole, **133**

chicken chili casserole, **134**

SMOTHERED CHICKEN AND GRAVY

1 (3-pound) chicken (cut into serving-size pieces)

2 teaspoons salt

1/2 teaspoon pepper

1/2 cup vegetable oil

3/4 cup all-purpose flour

3 cups water

1 (.87-ounce) package brown gravy mix

Wash chicken and place on paper towels to drain. Blot excess liquid. Sprinkle with salt and pepper. Heat oil in a large skillet. Set aside 1 Tablespoon flour for later use. While oil is heating, dredge chicken in flour, one piece at a time. Drop each piece of chicken in hot oil as soon as coated with flour. Brown chicken on both sides. Turn pieces at least twice to assure even browning. (Chicken does not need to be thoroughly cooked at this time since additional cooking is required.) Remove pieces from skillet. Place on paper towels to drain. Remove all but 2 Tablespoons grease from pan. Leave crusty pieces from chicken in skillet.

Reheat remaining grease. Stir in 1 Tablespoon flour. Quickly blend flour into hot grease. Stir until mixture is light to medium brown. Pour 2 cups water into skillet. Return chicken pieces to skillet. In a small mixing bowl, combine gravy mix and 1 cup warm water. Remove all lumps from mixture. Pour liquid into skillet. Cover with tight-fitting lid.

Simmer 30-40 minutes.

Add additional water, as needed, for desired consistency.

EASY BAKED CHICKEN AND GRAVY

1 (3-4 pound) fryer
1 teaspoon paprika
1/2 teaspoon salt
1/2 teaspoon garlic salt
1/2 teaspoon celery salt
1/4 teaspoon red pepper
1 (10-1/4-ounce) can cream of chicken soup
1 (.87-ounce) package brown gravy mix
3/4 cup water
1/4 cup grated Parmesan cheese

Cut chicken into serving size pieces. Remove skin. Wash chicken and let dry. Place pieces on a cutting board.

Combine all seasonings. Mix well. Sprinkle over chicken. Place in a greased 9x9-inch baking dish.

In a small saucepan, combine cream of chicken soup, gravy mix, water, and Parmesan cheese. Heat thoroughly. Beat with wire whisk for creamy texture. Pour heated mixture over chicken. Cover with a tight-fitting lid.

Bake at 375 degrees - 40 minutes. Uncover and bake 15 additional minutes. Cover and let set in oven 10 additional minutes after baking.

Zama, who is now eighty-two years old, continues to tend half a dozen chickens on her small farm. "As a young child, my favorite chore was gathering eggs. For me, finding an egg in a nest was magical and thrilling. I went through all kinds of rituals to make certain that the hens were 'happy' enough to keep producing. I was convinced that they laid eggs only because I decorated the nests and sang silly songs to them."

SPICY SOUTHERN FRIED CHICKEN

1 (3-pound) fryer
(cut into serving
size pieces)
2 cups buttermilk
2 eggs
1 Tablespoon
Worcestershire
sauce
1 Tablespoon Creole
seasoning
1 pound shortening
1/4 cup butter
1-1/2 cups all-purpose
flour
3 teaspoons salt
2 teaspoons paprika
1 teaspoon white
pepper
1 teaspoon black
pepper
1/2 teaspoon cayenne
pepper

Wash chicken and place on paper towels to dry. In a large mixing bowl, combine buttermilk, eggs, Worcestershire sauce, and Creole seasoning. Whisk to blend. Add chicken to mixture and toss to coat. Refrigerate 2-3 hours. (May be left overnight.)

Heat shortening and butter to 350 degrees in a cast-iron skillet. (Temperature may be checked by dropping a pinch of flour into hot oil. Oil should sizzle or bubble around flour when ready for frying.)

While oil is heating, combine remaining dry ingredients in a brown or plastic bag. Remove chicken from liquid. Drop one piece at a time into bag and shake vigorously to coat with flour. Drop chicken into hot oil. Maintain temperature at 310 - 320 degrees while cooking. Do not crowd chicken pieces into skillet. Turn frequently while cooking. Cooking time will vary from 18-25 minutes.

To check for doneness of chicken, make a small incision next to bone on a piece of dark meat.

OVEN FRIED CHICKEN

1 (2-3 pound) fryer
2 cups buttermilk
1/4 cup Worcestershire
   sauce
1 Tablespoon lemon
   juice
1 Tablespoon soy
   sauce
2 teaspoons hot sauce
2 cloves garlic
   (minced)
1-1/2 cups plain
   breadcrumbs
1/4 cup grated
   Parmesan cheese
1 Tablespoon dried
   parsley
1 teaspoon paprika
1 teaspoon salt
1/2 teaspoon black
   pepper
1/8 teaspoon red
   pepper
1 stick butter

Cut fryer into serving-size pieces. Wash and drain chicken.

Combine liquid ingredients with garlic. Whisk to blend. Pour over chicken. (Chicken should be in a glass bowl.) Let set in refrigerator several hours.

When ready to cook, combine breadcrumbs, cheese, parsley, and seasonings. Mix well. Spread mixture in a long flat pan. Remove chicken from buttermilk. Dredge chicken pieces in breadcrumb mixture to coat. Place chicken pieces on lightly greased baking sheet.

Drizzle melted butter over chicken.

Bake at 325 degrees - 25 minutes. Turn chicken pieces. Bake additional 20 minutes. Let chicken set at least 15 minutes before serving.

GARLIC BAKED CHICKEN

1 (3-pound) chicken
2 Tablespoons Creole
   seasoning
40 cloves garlic
   (unpeeled)
1 small bell pepper
   (cut into strips)
1 onion (sliced into
   1/2-inch wedges)
1 fresh lemon (sliced)
1/2 cup dry white wine
1/4 cup melted butter

Wash and pat dry chicken. Rub Creole seasoning over entire surface and inside cavity of chicken. Stuff cavity with 5 cloves of garlic, bell pepper, onion, and sliced lemon. Tie drumsticks together with twine.

Place chicken on a rack in a roasting pan. Arrange remaining garlic around chicken in pan.

Bake at 375 degrees - 25 minutes.

Combine wine and melted butter. Whisk vigorously to blend. Pour over chicken. Bake additional 45 minutes. Baste frequently after wine has been poured over chicken. Discard stuffing and garlic pieces before serving.

OVEN-BARBECUED CHICKEN

1 (2-3 pound) fryer (quartered)
1 teaspoon Creole seasoning
1 Tablespoon all-purpose flour
1 cup catsup
1 small onion (finely chopped)
1/4 cup firmly packed brown sugar
2 Tablespoons white wine vinegar
2 Tablespoons Worcestershire sauce
2 Tablespoons mustard

Remove skin from chicken. Wash and dry with paper towels. Sprinkle with seasoning. Place pieces of chicken in a greased 13x9x2-inch glass baking dish.

In a small saucepan, combine remaining ingredients. Whisk to blend thoroughly. Heat until first boiling bubble breaks surface. Let cool to lukewarm. Pour sauce over chicken. Cover with foil.

Bake at 350 degrees - 30 minutes. Uncover and bake additional 30 minutes.

EASY BAKED CHICKEN LOAF

3 cups cooked chopped chicken
1 cup soft bread crumbs
2 Tablespoons chopped celery
2 Tablespoons chopped parsley
1 teaspoon salt
1 teaspoon pepper
1/2 teaspoon onion salt
2 eggs (beaten)
1 cup milk
3 Tablespoons melted butter
2 Tablespoons dry breadcrumbs

Combine all ingredients. Mix well. Coat pan with butter. Pour mixture into an 8-inch loaf pan. Sprinkle dry breadcrumbs over loaf.

Bake at 350 degrees - 30 minutes.

STUFFED CHICKEN BREAST
(w/crab sauce)

6 boneless chicken breasts

1/4 cup margarine (melted)

3 Tablespoons paprika

2 teaspoons Creole seasoning

1/2 teaspoon garlic powder

1/2 teaspoon pepper

1/4 teaspoon salt

3/4 cup cooked ground pork sausage

1 (6-ounce) box stuffing mix

Pound chicken breasts with a wooden mallet to flatten.

Combine melted margarine and seasonings. Spoon over chicken breasts. Set aside.

Grind sausage in a food processor for extra fine texture. Prepare stuffing according to package directions. Add sausage. Spoon stuffing along center of breasts. Roll up and secure with toothpicks. Place stuffed breasts (seam side down) in a greased pan.

Bake at 400 degrees - 25-30 minutes.

CRAB SAUCE

1 stick margarine

1/4 cup chopped onion

3 Tablespoons all-purpose flour

1-1/2 cups chicken broth

1 teaspoon salt

1/2 teaspoon white pepper

2 bay leaves

1 (6-ounce) can crab meat

Melt margarine in a small skillet. Sauté onion 2 minutes. Stir in flour until blended (3-4 minutes). Add broth. Blend until creamy. Add remaining ingredients.

Simmer 10-15 minutes. Remove bay leaves.

Spoon hot sauce over stuffed breasts.

DISH PAN CHICKEN AND CORNBREAD DRESSING

1 (3-pound) fryer (quartered)

8 cups water

1 large bell pepper (cut into strips)

1 bunch celery (cut into 4-inch lengths)

1 large onion (peeled & halved)

2 pounds hot ground sausage

5 cups crumbled cornbread

4 cups cracker crumbs

1 (6-ounce) package stove top dressing

4 boiled eggs (finely chopped)

2 Tablespoons mustard

2 Tablespoons mayonnaise

2 teaspoons salt

2 teaspoons pepper

1/2 teaspoon sage

1/4 teaspoon red pepper

1/4 teaspoon garlic powder

In a large Dutch oven, cover chicken with water. Add vegetables. Bring mixture to a rolling boil. Cook over medium heat until chicken is tender enough to easily separate from bone. Remove chicken from broth. Set aside to cool. Remove vegetables from broth and discard, reserving all broth for later use. Remove bones from chicken and chop into small pieces.

Brown sausage in a large skillet. (Make sure that sausage does not clump together while browning.) Drain excess grease. In a very large mixing bowl or dish pan, combine all remaining ingredients. Mix well. Add broth, 1 cup at a time, until dressing is slightly soupy. (Excess liquid will be absorbed during baking.)

Bake at 350 degrees - 30 minutes or until dressing becomes slightly crusty on outer edges.

Additional broth may be poured over dressing while baking if mixture is too dry. Dressing may be frozen for several weeks before baking.

CHICKEN AND CORNBREAD CASSEROLE

1 (2-1/2-pound) fryer (quartered)

1 small onion (finely chopped)

2 teaspoons Creole seasoning

5 Tablespoons butter

3/4 cup flour

3 cups chicken broth

1-3/4 cups evaporated milk

3/4 cup yellow cornmeal

1 Tablespoon baking powder

2 Tablespoons sugar

1 egg

2 Tablespoons vegetable oil

1 Tablespoon Worcestershire sauce

1/2 teaspoon salt

1/2 teaspoon pepper

1/2 teaspoon garlic

1 cup grated Cheddar cheese

Cover chicken and onion with water. Add Creole seasoning. Cook until chicken is tender. Remove from liquid and reserve broth. Bone and chop chicken into large pieces.

Melt butter in a medium saucepan. Stir flour into butter. Add broth and milk. Gradually stir in cornmeal, baking powder, and sugar.

In a small bowl, combine egg, vegetable oil, Worcestershire sauce, and seasonings. Whisk to blend. Add to cornmeal mixture. Stir in chicken and cheese. Mix well. Spoon into a greased 3-quart baking dish. Cover.

Bake at 350 degrees 20 minutes. Uncover and bake additional 15 minutes or until golden brown.

MOZZARELLA CHICKEN WITH RED SAUCE

12 ounces angel hair
  pasta
2 Tablespoons butter
6 boneless chicken
  breasts
1 teaspoon salt
1/2 teaspoon white
  pepper
1 cup Italian bread-
  crumbs
1/2 cup olive oil

Cook pasta according to package directions. Drain thoroughly and toss with butter.

Wash chicken and place on paper towels to drain. Sprinkle salt and white pepper over both sides of chicken. Dredge breasts in breadcrumbs. Lightly brown in hot oil on both sides. Transfer breasts to a greased baking dish.

SAUCE

2 (15-ounce) cans
  Italian tomato sauce
2 cups water
1/2 teaspoon sugar
1/2 teaspoon sweet basil
1/2 teaspoon oregano
1/2 teaspoon garlic
  powder
1/2 teaspoon salt
1/2 teaspoon black
  pepper
3 Tablespoons white
  wine
6 thin slices Mozzarella
  cheese
1 teaspoon dried parsley

Pour Italian tomato sauce, water, sugar, and seasonings into a large saucepan. Simmer 10 minutes. Add wine and simmer additional 10 minutes. Pour sauce over chicken breasts. Cover to bake.

Bake at 300 degrees 35 minutes. Baste several times while baking.

Remove from oven. Cover each breast with a cheese slice. Sprinkle with parsley. Serve over pasta.

poultry

CHICKEN NOODLE CASSEROLE

1 (7-ounce) box thin
  macaroni noodles
1 (3-pound) fryer
  (cut into serving-
  size pieces)
6 Tablespoons
  margarine
5 Tablespoons flour
4 cups broth
1 cup half & half
1 teaspoon paprika
1 teaspoon salt
1/2 teaspoon black
  pepper
1/4 teaspoon red
  pepper
3/4 cup Italian bread-
  crumbs
1-1/2 cups grated
  Cheddar cheese

Cook noodles according to package directions. Drain and rinse in cold water.

Cover chicken with water. Cook on high heat until chicken easily separates from bone (approximately 45 minutes). Remove from broth, reserving broth for later use. Bone chicken and chop into small pieces.

In a large saucepan, melt margarine. Blend in flour. Stir in broth and milk. Add seasonings and remove from heat. (Do not allow mixture to thicken.) Fold chicken, noodles, and 3/4 cup cheese into mixture. Pour into a greased 2-quart casserole dish. Cover during baking.

Bake at 350 degrees - 45 minutes.

Combine breadcrumbs and remaining cheese. Sprinkle over hot casserole. Return to oven for 10 additional minutes. Leave uncovered. Remove from oven. Let set 20 minutes before serving.

OVERNIGHT CHICKEN CASSEROLE

1 (12-inch) loaf sour dough bread

1 Tablespoon butter

1-1/2 cups finely chopped onion

1/4 cup finely chopped green onion

1/4 cup finely chopped green pepper

5 chicken breasts (cooked & chopped)

1/2 cup mayonnaise

1 Tablespoon instant chicken bouillon granules

2 teaspoons Creole seasoning

3/4 teaspoon pepper

4 eggs (beaten)

3 cups milk

1 (10-3/4-ounce) can cream of mushroom soup

1 cup grated Cheddar cheese

Freeze bread for 30 minutes. Remove and cut into 1/2-inch cubes. Layer 1/2 bread in a large greased baking dish.

Sauté onions and green pepper in butter until vegetables are tender. (Do not brown.) Stir in chicken, mayonnaise, bouillon, and seasonings. Spoon mixture over bread cubes. Layer remaining bread over mixture. Combine eggs and milk. Whisk to blend thoroughly. Pour liquid over casserole. Cover with tight-fitting lid. Refrigerate overnight. Uncover to bake.

Bake at 350 degrees - 15 minutes.

Spread soup over casserole.

Bake 35 minutes. Sprinkle with cheese. Bake additional 10 minutes.

CHICKEN VEGETABLE SKILLET

1 (2-1/2-pound) fryer
1 teaspoon salt
1/2 teaspoon pepper
1/2 teaspoon sweet basil
1 stick margarine
2 cloves garlic (minced)
1 Tablespoon green chili
   peppers
1 small bell pepper
   (cut into 1-inch strips)
1 small onion
   (sliced into rings)
2 cups frozen corn
1 (15-1/4-ounce) can Italian
   stewed tomatoes
1/4 cup water

Cut chicken into serving-size pieces. Sprinkle with seasonings. Melt margarine in a large skillet. Brown chicken in margarine. Layer vegetables over chicken in order listed. Pour Italian tomatoes and water over chicken and vegetables. Cover and simmer 35 minutes or until vegetables are tender.

Additional water may be added (1/4 cup at a time).

CHICKEN AND WILD RICE DISH

4 chicken breasts (cut into
   long strips)
4 Tablespoons butter
1/4 cup finely chopped onion
1/4 cup finely chopped green
   onion
1/4 cup finely chopped black
   olives
2 cups chicken broth
1 cup water
1 (16-ounce) can Cajun-style
   tomatoes
1 (6-ounce) package long
   grain & wild rice

In a cast-iron pot, brown chicken strips and onions in butter. Add remaining ingredients. Bring mixture to a boil. Cover and reduce heat. Simmer 20 minutes.

Dish may be topped with 1/2 cup grated cheese.

CHICKEN ASPARAGUS CASSEROLE

6 chicken breasts
1/2 cup butter
3/4 cup chopped onion
1/4 cup chopped green pepper
1 Tablespoon flour
1 (10-3/4-ounce) can cream of mushroom soup
1 (10-3/4-ounce) can cream of chicken soup
3/4 cup evaporated milk
1 cup grated Cheddar cheese
1 Tablespoon soy sauce
1 teaspoon hot sauce
1 teaspoon salt
1/2 teaspoon pepper
2 (15-ounce) cans asparagus
3/4 cup slivered almonds (toasted)

Pan-fry chicken breasts in 6 Tablespoons melted butter. In a saucepan, melt remaining 2 Tablespoons butter. Sauté onion and green pepper until tender. Stir in flour to blend. Add soups, milk, cheese, soy sauce, hot sauce, and seasonings to pan. Heat thoroughly. Whisk vigorously until mixture is smooth. Heat until first boiling bubble breaks surface.

Place browned chicken in a 2-quart baking dish. Pour 1/2 sauce over chicken. (Keep remaining sauce warm.) Cover with foil.

Bake at 350 degrees - 15 minutes.

Remove from oven. Uncover and let set 15 minutes. Make a layer of asparagus. Pour remaining sauce over asparagus. Sprinkle with toasted almonds.

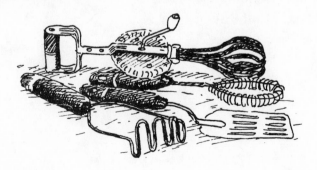

CHICKEN CHILI CASSEROLE

2/3 cup rice
1 (14-1/2-ounce) can chicken broth
4 cups cooked and chopped chicken
1 (10-3/4-ounce) can cream of chicken soup
1 (10-3/4-ounce) can cream of mushroom soup
1 (8-ounce) jar taco sauce
2 cups frozen whole kernel corn (thawed)
1 small onion (finely chopped)
1 Tablespoon Worcestershire sauce
2 teaspoons chili powder
1 teaspoon oregano
1 teaspoon garlic powder
1/2 teaspoon pepper
1 cup grated Monterey Jack cheese
1/2 cup plain bread-crumbs

Combine rice and chicken broth. Bring to a boil. Cover and simmer 25 minutes or until all liquid is absorbed.

Combine remaining ingredients, except cheese and breadcrumbs. Stir in rice. Mix well. Spoon mixture into a greased 2-quart baking dish. Sprinkle with cheese and breadcrumbs.

Bake at 350 degrees - 30 minutes. Uncover and bake 15 additional minutes.

meats
casseroles

*S*tanding alone on a dusty road, the general store hummed with activity. Outside, in the warm months, old-timers, perched on benches running along the porch, whittled away the hours while chewing tobacco and swapping stories about the weather, a new litter of pigs, a prize colt, or other community happenings. Their idle chatter was punctuated by the slamming of the screen door as youngsters darted in and out. The kids would make a bee-line for the ice cream box for a nickel dip of cream or rush to the soft drink box and plunge their hands into the slushy ice searching for a Nehi or Grapette drink. Occasionally, enough money remained for a Moon Pie or a Stage Plank. Mama was silent and slow compared to the men and the children. She paid attention to her list and the goods before her.

The store's walls were decorated with randomly hung signs advertising the merchandise most in demand. RC Cola, Martha White Flour, Hadocol's Cough Syrup, and Garret's Snuff were prominent items. The store's inventory rested on shelves, on and under counters, and in barrels and crates. Every nook, corner, and cranny housed plowpoints, harnesses, hardware, cookware, clothing, sewing thread, bolts of cloth, liniment, crackers, hoop cheese, and an assortment of other goods.

After Mama had the necessities, she would linger in the cloth section to admire the new prints. She touched the fabric again and again, such a smooth contrast to the starched "feed sack" floral she wore. She dreamed of the next visit when she would have enough egg money to buy material for a new Sunday dress. Before she left, she remembered to use the telephone, the only one for miles around.

The country store was a hive of activity: the grocery, the source of household and farm needs, a veterinary supply, the drugstore, service station, and post office. Visits there are sweet recall, the honey of remembrance.

meats and casseroles

company roast and gravy, 138

pot roast, 139

uncle nabob's beef stew, 140

creole baked steak, 141

meat balls and gravy, 142

meat loaf deluxe, 143

border beef delight, 144

beefy enchiladas, 145

macaroni and beef casserole, 146

lasagna quick, 147

spaghetti bake, 148

easy spicy chili, 149

glazed pork loin, 150

oven-barbecued pork ribs, 151

vegetable smothered pork chops, 152

pork chop casserole, 153

ham and vegetable pasta, 154

sausage and tortellini, 155

old-fashioned macaroni and cheese, 156

COMPANY ROAST AND GRAVY

1 (4-5 pound) rump roast

4 cloves garlic (minced)

1 Tablespoon Creole seasoning

3 Tablespoons all-purpose flour

1/4 cup cooking oil

1 (10-3/4-ounce) can cream of mushroom soup

3 cups water

1 (.87-ounce) package brown gravy mix

Make several 1/2-inch slits 4-5 inches apart over surface of roast. Stuff with garlic. Rub surface of meat with Creole seasoning. Cover roast with coating of flour. Heat oil in Dutch oven. When oil is sizzling, brown all sides of roast. Remove from pot. Add soup and water. Bring mixture to boil. Lower garlic stuffed roast into mixture. Cover with tight-fitting lid.

Bake at 300 degrees - 2 hours. Baste occasionally.

Dissolve gravy mix in 3/4 cup liquid from roast. Pour mixture over roast. Cook additional 45 minutes. (Cooking time may vary depending on desired tenderness.)

Additional water may be added for thinner gravy.

In the absence of weather reporting, "old timers" observed nature to predict patterns in weather. This body of information has become a part of the Southern folklore that is still considered as a reliable source of weather prediction.

POT ROAST

4 pound boneless chuck roast

2 teaspoons Creole seasoning

1/2 teaspoon garlic powder

1/4 teaspoon celery salt

1-1/4 teaspoons sweet basil

3 Tablespoons all-purpose flour

1-1/4 cups vegetable oil

1 (14.5-ounce) can beef broth

1/2 cup tomato juice

1/2 cup water

1 Tablespoon Worcestershire sauce

1 teaspoon teriyaki

1 onion (cut into thin rings)

2 carrots (cut into 2-inch pieces)

4 medium red potatoes (cut into quarters)

1/4 cup fresh parsley

Combine seasonings. Rub over surface of roast. Dredge in flour. Brown in hot oil. Drain excess oil.

Add broth, tomato juice, water, Worcestershire sauce, and teriyaki. Cover with tight-fitting lid. Simmer 1 hour. (Longer cooking time may be needed to reach desired tenderness.)

Add vegetables. Cover and simmer additional 45 minutes or until vegetables are tender. Cook uncovered last 10-15 minutes.

Garnish with parsley before serving.

Add water as needed. No more than 1/4 cup should be added at one time.

UNCLE NABOB'S BEEF STEW

3 pounds boneless
   top round steak
   (cut into 2-inch
   cubes)

2 teaspoons paprika

4 Tablespoons flour

4 Tablespoons
   vegetable oil

1 small onion
   (chopped)

2 cloves garlic
   (minced)

1 Tablespoon
   Worcestershire
   sauce

1 teaspoon dried
   parsley

1 teaspoon salt

1/4 teaspoon black
   pepper

1/4 teaspoon red
   pepper

1/4 teaspoon garlic
   salt

5 cups water

6 tender carrots
   (scrapped & cut
   into 3-inch
   pieces)

4 medium red
   potatoes (peeled
   & cubed)

Sprinkle paprika over meat. Dredge in flour to lightly coat. Heat oil in a heavy pot until sizzling hot. Brown meat on all sides. Halfway through the browning process, add onion and garlic to meat. Drain excess grease. Sprinkle with parsley and seasonings. Add water. Cover and simmer 1 hour (or until meat is tender).

Add carrots and potatoes. Cover. Cook over medium-low heat 30 minutes or until vegetables are tender. (Do not overcook vegetables.) Add additional water, if needed.

To thicken gravy, combine 3/4 cup hot water with 1 Tablespoon flour. Make a thin, smooth paste. Pour into stew and simmer 10 minutes.

CREOLE BAKED STEAK

2 pounds round steak
1 teaspoon salt
1/2 teaspoon black
    pepper
1/2 cup Italian bread
    crumbs
1/3 cup olive oil
2 Tablespoons butter
3/4 cup finely
    chopped onion
1/4 cup finely
    chopped green
    pepper
1/4 cup fresh
    chopped parsley
2 (15-ounce) cans
    Italian tomatoes
2 Tablespoons
    Worcestershire
    sauce
1/4 teaspoon red
    pepper
1/2 teaspoon sweet
    basil
1/2 teaspoon oregano
1/2 teaspoon garlic
    salt

Pound steak several times on both sides with meat mallet to tenderize. Sprinkle with salt and black pepper. Rub into surface of meat. Cut steak into 4 x 2-inch strips. Brown in oil and butter. Transfer to a 13x9x2-inch greased baking dish.

Remove all but 1 Tablespoon of oil from pan. Sauté onion, green pepper, and parsley in same pan used to brown meat. Add remaining ingredients to vegetables. Simmer 10 minutes. Pour sauce over steak. Cover.

Bake at 325 degrees - 1 hour 15 minutes or until meat is tender. Uncover last 10 minutes of baking time.

Serve over hot buttered noodles.

"Signs of Nature"
Flocks of blackbirds hovering close together near the ground means bad weather is coming.

141

MEATBALLS AND GRAVY

2 pounds ground beef
1/4 cup plain bread crumbs
1 Tablespoon flour
1 teaspoon Creole seasoning
1/2 teaspoon salt
1/2 teaspoon garlic powder
1/2 teaspoon onion powder
1/4 cup shortening

Combine meat, breadcrumbs, flour, and seasonings. Mix thoroughly. Form mixture into 1-1/2-inch meatballs. Brown in shortening. Drain excess grease.

GRAVY

2 cups water
2 (.87-ounce) packages brown gravy mix
1 Tablespoon instant roux and gravy mix
1 teaspoon browning and seasoning sauce

Heat ingredients in a small saucepan. Pour hot liquid over meatballs. Cover.

Simmer 30 minutes.

"Signs of Nature"
Harvested ears of corn with a heavy covering of silk indicate a severe winter is on its way.

MEAT LOAF DELUXE

1 Tablespoon butter

1/2 cup finely chopped onion

1/2 teaspoon garlic powder

3/4 cup evaporated milk

1 pound ground beef

1/2 cup chili sauce

1/2 pound ground sausage

2 Tablespoons steak sauce

1 egg (beaten)

1 cup herb-flavored stuffing mix

1 teaspoon salt

1 cup grated Cheddar cheese

1/2 teaspoon pepper

Sauté onion in butter until clear. Combine remaining ingredients in order listed. Mix thoroughly. Spoon into greased 9x5x2-inch loaf pan.

Bake at 350 degrees - 1 hour 15 minutes or until juices are no longer pink.

BORDER BEEF DELIGHT

2 pounds ground beef
1/4 cup finely chopped onion
1 Tablespoon finely chopped jalapeño pepper
1 (1.25-ounce) package taco seasoning
3/4 cup water
1 (16-ounce) jar taco sauce
8 (6-inch) flour tortillas (cut into 2-inch strips)
1 cup grated Cheddar cheese
1 cup grated Monterey Jack cheese
1 (16-ounce) can refried beans
2 cups sour cream
1/3 cup finely chopped green onion
1/3 cup chopped black olives

Brown beef, onion, and jalapeño pepper in a large skillet. Drain excess fat. Stir in taco seasoning, water, and taco sauce. Simmer 10 minutes.

Cover bottom of a 13x9x2-inch greased casserole dish with tortilla strips. Spoon 1/2 meat mixture over tortillas. Sprinkle with 1/2 cheese. Make a 2nd layer of tortilla strips. In a separate bowl, combine beans and sour cream. Beat to blend. Spread evenly over top layer. Sprinkle green onion and olives over mixture. Use remaining tortilla in next layer. Cover with 1/2 meat mixture. Top with remaining 1/2 cheese.

Bake at 350 degrees - 25-30 minutes.

Let set 15 minutes before serving.

"Signs of Nature"
Erratic behavior from animals during the day signals severe weather changes.

BEEFY ENCHILADAS

1 pound ground beef
1/2 cup finely
  chopped onion
1 (1-1/3-ounce) pack-
  age chili seasoning
1 (8-ounce) can
  tomato sauce
1 (8-ounce) can
  tomato paste
3/4 cup refried beans
3/4 cup water
1 (16-ounce) jar
  picante sauce
8 (6-inch) flour
  tortillas
2 cups grated
  Cheddar cheese
1 cup grated Monterey
  Jack cheese

Brown beef and onion in a heavy skillet. Drain thoroughly. Add chili seasoning, tomato sauce, tomato paste, refried beans, and water. Mix well. Simmer over low heat 15 minutes.

Pour picante sauce over bottom of a greased baking dish.

Spread meat mixture over center of each tortilla. Sprinkle 1 Tablespoon Cheddar cheese down center of mixture. Loosely roll tortillas. Arrange seam side down in a baking dish over picante sauce. Sprinkle remaining cheese over enchiladas.

Bake at 325 degrees - 15-20 minutes.

MACARONI AND BEEF CASSEROLE

1 pound ground beef
3/4 cup chopped onion
2 teaspoons minced
   garlic
2 (8-ounce) cans
   tomato sauce
1 teaspoon salt
1/2 teaspoon pepper
1/2 teaspoon oregano
1/2 teaspoon sweet
   basil
1 (7-ounce) box small
   elbow macaroni
2 cups grated Cheddar
   cheese
1 egg (beaten)
3 Tablespoons
   margarine
3 Tablespoons all-
   purpose flour
1-1/2 cups milk

Brown beef, onion, and garlic until vegetables are tender. Thoroughly drain meat. Add tomato sauce and seasonings. Simmer 12 minutes.

Cook macaroni according to package directions. Drain. Stir in egg and 1 cup cheese. Toss until cheese melts.

In a medium saucepan, melt margarine and blend in flour. Add milk and cook over medium, stirring constantly until mixture thickens. Add remaining cheese. Whisk to blend until cheese melts.

In a greased 13x9x2-inch baking dish, layer 1/2 macaroni. Top with meat mixture. Make another layer of macaroni. Spoon cheese sauce over casserole.

Bake at 350 degrees - 30 minutes or until top begins to brown.

Let set at least 15 minutes before serving.

LASAGNA QUICK

2 pounds ground beef

3/4 cup finely chopped onion

2 cloves garlic (minced)

2 Tablespoons olive oil

1 (8-ounce) can tomato sauce

2 (14.5-ounce) cans chopped Italian tomatoes

1-1/2 teaspoons salt

1/2 teaspoon pepper

1/2 teaspoon oregano

1/2 teaspoon sweet basil

1 teaspoon sugar

1 (12-ounce) package lasagna noodles

8 ounces Mozzarella cheese (grated)

12 ounces Ricotta cheese

2/3 cup Parmesan cheese (grated)

Brown beef and vegetables in olive oil. Drain thoroughly. Add tomato sauce, tomatoes, seasonings, and sugar. Leave uncovered and simmer 30 minutes.

Cook noodles according to package directions. Rinse in warm water. Make a layer of noodles in a 13x9x2-inch glass casserole dish.

Combine cheeses. Alternately layer meat sauce, cheeses, and noodles.

Bake at 375 degrees - 25 minutes.

"Signs of Nature"
When root crops like onions and sweet potatoes have thicker skins, a cold winter is forecast.

SPAGHETTI BAKE

12 ounces spaghetti

2 Tablespoons butter

2 pounds ground meat

1/2 cup finely chopped onion

1/4 cup finely chopped green pepper

2 cloves garlic (minced)

1 (15-ounce) can chopped tomatoes w/liquid

1 (15-ounce) can tomato sauce

1 (8-ounce) can tomato paste

2 teaspoons sugar

1 (4-ounce) can mushrooms (drained)

1 (4-ounce) can black olives (drained)

1 teaspoon salt

1 teaspoon pepper

1 teaspoon oregano

1/2 teaspoon sweet basil

1 cup grated Mozzarella cheese

1 cup grated Cheddar cheese

1/2 cup Parmesan cheese (grated)

Cook spaghetti according to package directions. Drain and toss with butter.

Brown beef, onion, pepper, and garlic in a heavy skillet. Drain excess fat. Stir in tomato ingredients, sugar, mushrooms, olives, and seasonings.

Combine cheeses. Layer 1/2 spaghetti in a 13x9x2-inch casserole dish. Spoon 1/2 meat sauce over layer. Sprinkle 1/2 cheese mixture over sauce. Repeat layers.

Bake at 375 degrees - 30 minutes.

EASY SPICY CHILI

1 pound ground meat
3 cloves garlic
   (minced)
1 cup finely chopped
   onion
1/2 cup finely chopped
   bell pepper
4 Tablespoons chili
   powder
1 teaspoon salt
1/2 teaspoon garlic
   powder
1/2 teaspoon oregano
1 (14-1/2-ounce) can
   stewed tomatoes
1 (10-ounce) can
   Rotel tomatoes
1 (8-ounce) can
   tomato sauce
1 cup water
1 (15-ounce) can
   pinto beans

Brown meat, garlic, onion, and bell pepper. Drain excess fat from meat.

Add remaining ingredients, except beans to meat mixture. Bring mixture to a boil. Cook on high heat 10 minutes. Cover and simmer 30 minutes.

Add beans and simmer additional 30 minutes.

GLAZED PORK LOIN

1 (4-5-pound) pork
  roast
1 teaspoon mustard
1/2 teaspoon salt
1/2 teaspoon black
  pepper
1/2 teaspoon Creole
  seasoning
1/2 teaspoon garlic
  powder
1/4 teaspoon sage
1/2 cup vegetable oil
1/2 cup water

Combine mustard and seasonings. Rub over surface of roast. In
a cast-iron pot, brown all sides of
roast in sizzling hot oil. Drain oil
from pot. Add 1/2 cup water.
Cover with tight fitting lid.

Bake at 400 degrees 15 minutes.
Reduce temperature to 325 degrees
and bake additional 2 hours.

*Add 1/3 cup water at 30-minute inter-
vals.*

SAUCE
1 cup mayhaw jelly
1 small apple (finely
  chopped)
1/2 cup orange juice
1/3 cup lemon juice
1/2 cup red wine
1/2 teaspoon white
  pepper
1/4 teaspoon black
  pepper
2 Tablespoons corn-
  starch

Combine all ingredients, except
cornstarch, in a small saucepan.
Simmer 15 minutes. Remove 1/2
cup liquid from pan. Stir cornstarch into mixture until blended.
Pour mixture into hot liquid.
Simmer until mixture thickens
(approximately 10 minutes). Stir
constantly to prevent scorching.

Remove roast from oven and
spoon sauce over roast. Leave
roast uncovered and return to
oven for 20 minutes.

OVEN-BARBECUED PORK RIBS

4 pounds lean pork ribs

1 teaspoon salt

1/2 teaspoon black pepper

1/2 teaspoon garlic powder

1/2 teaspoon onion powder

1/4 teaspoon celery salt

1/4 cup vegetable oil

1/3 cup catsup

1/3 cup apple cider vinegar

1/2 cup brown sugar

2 Tablespoons Worcestershire sauce

1 Tablespoon soy sauce

1 teaspoon ginger

1 teaspoon Louisiana hot sauce

1/4 teaspoon red pepper

Combine seasonings. Rub seasonings over entire surface of ribs. Brown ribs in hot oil. Remove from oil and place ribs in a baking dish. Cover.

Make a sauce from remaining ingredients. Heat thoroughly. Pour sauce over ribs.

Bake at 450 degrees - 15 minutes. Reduce heat to 325 degrees. Bake 1 hour or until ribs are tender. Baste occasionally.

"Signs of Nature"
When the goldenrods bloom, the first frost will come in six weeks.

VEGETABLE SMOTHERED PORK CHOPS

5 lean pork chops
1/2 teaspoon pepper
1/2 teaspoon Creole seasoning
1/4 cup cooking oil
4 yellow squash (cut into 1/4-inch slices)
2 large zucchini (cut into 1/4-inch slices)
1 large onion (chopped)
1 cup green onions (chopped)
1 large green pepper (cut into 1-inch strips)
1 large red pepper (cut into 1-inch strips)
1 large yellow pepper (cut into 1-inch strips)
1 (14.5-ounce) can stewed tomatoes
1 (10-ounce) can Rotel tomatoes
1/2 cup water
1 teaspoon sugar
1/2 teaspoon garlic powder
1/2 teaspoon oregano

Sprinkle pork chops with pepper and Creole seasoning. Brown chops in hot oil. Remove from oil. Place pork chops in a large heavy pot or skillet.

Layer vegetables over pork chops.

Combine remaining ingredients. Pour mixture over vegetables. Cover and cook over medium heat 30 minutes. Stir occasionally to prevent sticking. Reduce heat and simmer 1-1/2 hours or until vegetables are tender.

PORK CHOP CASSEROLE

5 lean pork chops
1/2 teaspoon Creole
    seasoning
1/2 cup olive oil
3/4 cup rice
1 tomato (sliced)
1 small onion (sliced
    into rings)
1/2 bell pepper (cut
    into rings)
1/2 cup fresh sliced
    mushrooms
1 (14.5 ounce) can
    beef broth

Rub seasoning over surface of pork chops. Brown meat in hot oil. Drain and set aside.

Grease bottom of baking dish. Layer rice in dish. Place pork chops over top of rice. Layer vegetables over meat. Pour broth over vegetables. Cover dish.

Bake at 350 degrees - 1 hour.

"Signs of Nature"
Thick animal fur in fall means a severe winter is in store.

HAM AND VEGETABLE PASTA

8 ounces spiral
  macaroni
2 teaspoons olive oil
1 cup cooked ham (cut
  into 1/2-inch cubes)
1/4 cup finely chopped
  onion
1 (8-ounce) package
  frozen cauliflower
1 (8-ounce) package
  frozen green beans
2 Tablespoons butter
2 Tablespoons flour
1-1/2 cups milk
1-1/2 cups grated
  Cheddar cheese
1 teaspoon mustard
1/2 teaspoon salt
1/4 teaspoon white
  pepper
1/8 teaspoon red
  pepper

Prepare pasta according to package directions. Drain thoroughly. Toss with olive oil. Layer in a greased casserole dish.

Steam vegetables until tender. Add ham to cooked vegetables. Toss to mix.

Melt butter in a small saucepan. Stir in flour and blend over medium heat 2 minutes. Remove from heat. Gradually stir in milk. Whisk to blend thoroughly. Heat over medium heat until first boiling bubble breaks surface. Add 3/4 cup cheese, mustard, and seasonings. Add vegetables to cheese sauce. Pour over pasta. Top with remaining cheese.

Bake at 350 degrees - 15 minutes. Broil until browned.

"Signs of Nature"
Rain on Easter Sunday means rain for the next seven Sundays.

SAUSAGE AND TORTELLINI

1 pound hot smoked
   sausage (sliced
   into 1/2-inch
   wafers)
1 Tablespoon olive oil
1 (16-ounce) package
   tortellini
3 Tablespoons butter
2 teaspoons flour
1-1/3 cups half & half
1/2 teaspoon salt
1/4 teaspoon pepper
1/8 teaspoon nutmeg
1/4 cup grated
   Cheddar cheese
1/4 cup grated
   Parmesan cheese

Cook pasta according to package directions. Drain. Spoon into greased casserole dish.

Brown sausage in olive oil. Drain and set aside.

In a medium saucepan, melt butter. Stir in flour. Blend for 2 minutes. Slowly add half & half. Heat until mixture begins to thicken. Add seasonings and nutmeg. Add 1/4 cup combined cheeses to mixture. Add sausage. Pour mixture over pasta. Sprinkle remaining cheese mixture over sauce.

Broil at 425 degrees until mixture is browned slightly.

OLD-FASHIONED MACARONI AND CHEESE

2 cups macaroni
  (uncooked)
5 cups water
3 Tablespoons butter
10 ounces grated
  Cheddar cheese
1 egg
1-1/4 cups milk
1 teaspoon salt
1/2 teaspoon pepper
2/3 cup buttery
  cracker crumbs

Drop macaroni into boiling water. Cook over medium heat 7 minutes. Drain thoroughly. Toss noodles with butter. Layer 1/2 of noodles in a 1-1/2-quart greased casserole dish.

Set aside 2 Tablespoons cheese for topping. Sprinkle 1/2 of remaining cheese over macaroni. Repeat layer of noodles and cheese.

Combine egg, milk, salt, and pepper. Whisk to blend. Pour mixture over layers. Combine crackers and 2 Tablespoons cheese. Sprinkle over top of casserole.

Bake at 325 degrees - 35-40 minutes.

fish
seafood

*M*any past genera-
tions have enjoyed the
cool, clear, spring-fed
water of the old swim-
min' hole. The banks
were worn smooth and
slick by bare-footed
youngsters jumping into
and climbing hurriedly
from the grasp of bone-
chilling water.

During one summer
drought, the creek
stopped runnin' and the
spring slowed to a mere
trickle. Some of the
boys gathered feed
sacks from the commu-
nity and filled them
with sand to build a
dam. Soon the water
was deeper than ever.
This success was
encouragement enough
to add a diving board
and a single rope swing
to an outstretched limb
of a towering beech
tree.

Most every Sunday
afternoon, June through
August, was spent at the
old swimmin' hole.
Outgrown and always
worn cut-off overalls
served as swimsuits for
the boys if girls were
around. When the boys
were alone at the hole,
they usually went skin-
ny-dippin'. Someone
always stood watch to
keep pesky girls from
slipping up and run-
ning off with their
clothes.

The old swimmin'
hole served the com-
munity well: a water-
ing hole for stock, a
baptismal for the
church, and, some-
times, a fishing hole
offering a mess of
small perch for supper.
But mostly, it was a
place of fun and frolic.
With the passing of
time, the slick banks
have disappeared
under thick growths of
vines and brush. All
that remains of the old
swimmin' hole are
memories and a trickle
of cool water flowing
over roots of an old and
gnarled beech tree with
initials carved deep
into its bark.

seafood

ttuccine, *160*

mbalaya, *161*

casserole, *162*

awfish pie, *163*

atin, *164*

shrimp stuffed pasta rolls with cheese sauce, *165*

shrimp, chicken, and sausage favorite, *166*

shrimp and sausage spaghetti, *167*

pan-fried louisiana catfish with shrimp sauce, *168*

tangy baked catfish, *169*

baked catfish, *170*

pan-fried catfish cakes, *171*

seafood, sausage, and chicken gumbo, *172*

shrimp stew, *173*

fish stew, *174*

oyster stew, *175*

fish and seafood sauces, *176*

CRAWFISH FETTUCCINE

1 (12-ounce) package
  fettuccine
1 Tablespoon olive oil
2 teaspoons paprika
1 pound crawfish tails
1/4 cup butter
1/2 cup green onion
2 cloves garlic
  (minced)
1 teaspoon Creole
  seasoning
1/2 teaspoon celery
  salt
1/2 teaspoon salt
1/4 teaspoon pepper
1/8 teaspoon cayenne
2 cups half & half
1 Tablespoon all-
  purpose flour
1-1/4 cups process
  cheese
1 teaspoon dried
  parsley

Cook fettuccine according to package directions. Drain and toss with olive oil. Set aside.

Sprinkle crawfish with paprika. Melt butter in a large skillet. Sauté green onions 2 minutes. Add crawfish, garlic, and seasonings. Cover and simmer 8-10 minutes. Stir as needed to prevent sticking. Combine flour with 3/4 cup half & half to make a thin paste. Pour over crawfish. Mix well. Gradually pour remaining milk over mixture. Stir until well mixed. Add cheese and parsley. As soon as cheese melts, pour crawfish mixture over fettuccine. Toss to mix.

Long before commercial crawfish ponds became a profitable industry in Louisiana, youngsters fished for "crawdads" with a string and fat meat. During the hot summertime, they would finish their chores and spend hours filling buckets with "mud bugs."

CRAWFISH JAMBALAYA

1 pound smoked
sausage (cut into
1/4-inch slices)

3 Tablespoons cook-
ing oil

2 Tablespoons
all-purpose flour

1 cup finely chopped
onion

3/4 cup chopped
parsley

1/2 cup finely
chopped green
pepper

1/2 cup finely
chopped celery

3 cloves minced garlic

1 (14.5-ounce) can
chopped tomatoes
(with juice)

1 (8-ounce) can
tomato sauce

1 teaspoon Creole
seasoning

1 teaspoon salt

1/4 teaspoon cayenne
pepper

1 cup chicken broth

2-1/2 cups water

1 pound crawfish

2 cups long grain rice
(uncooked)

Lightly brown sausage in a large pot. Remove sausage and place on paper towels to drain.

Combine oil and flour in pot where sausage was browned. Blend thoroughly. Cook over medium heat, stirring constantly until mixture is golden brown. Add onion, parsley, green pepper, celery, and garlic to mixture. Cook until onions become transparent. Add tomatoes, tomato sauce, and seasonings. Simmer 10 minutes. Add broth and water. Stir in rice. Cover and simmer 10 minutes. Add sausage and crawfish. Cover and simmer until rice is tender (approximately 20 minutes).

Additional water may be used, if needed.

SPICY CRAWFISH CASSEROLE

1 (8-ounce) package
  long grain and wild
  rice

2 green onions (finely
  chopped)

2 Tablespoons butter

1 (3-ounce) package
  cream cheese

1 (16-ounce) package
  crawfish tails

1 teaspoon paprika

1 cup grated Cheddar
  cheese

1 (10-3/4-ounce) can
  chicken & mush-
  room soup

1/2 cup milk

1 Tablespoon
  Worcestershire
  sauce

1 teaspoon Creole
  seasoning

1/8 teaspoon cayenne
  pepper

Prepare rice mix according to package directions.

Sauté onions in butter until wilted. Stir in cream cheese. Combine remaining ingredients in order listed. Fold in rice. Mix thoroughly. Spoon mixture into greased 2 quart baking dish. Cover.

Bake at 350 degrees - 50 minutes.

ME-OH-MY-OH CRAWFISH PIE

1 small onion (chopped)
2/3 cup chopped celery
1/3 cup chopped bell
pepper
3/4 cup butter
1 pound crawfish tails
1 teaspoon paprika
1/2 cup chopped green
onion
1/3 cup minced parsley
1 Tablespoon chopped
jalapeño pepper
1 teaspoon Creole
seasoning
1/2 teaspoon salt
1/4 teaspoon garlic
powder
1/2 cup milk
1 Tablespoon cornstarch
1 Tablespoon tomato
sauce
1 Tablespoon lemon juice
1/2 cup seasoned bread-
crumbs
2 (9-inch) pastry shells

Sauté onion, celery, and bell pepper in butter until tender. Add crawfish, paprika, green onion, parsley, jalapeño pepper, and seasonings. Cook on medium heat 4-5 minutes. Add milk, cornstarch, tomato sauce, and lemon juice, stirring until mixture begins to thicken. Remove from heat. Let mixture cool 10 minutes.

Fold in breadcrumbs. Pour filling into piecrust. Arrange top crust over filling and pinch sides to seal. Cut (3) 1-inch slits in the top of crust.

Bake at 425 degrees 7 minutes, then lower to 375 degrees and bake for 35 minutes.

Leener was six or seven years old when Grannie and PawPaw took her fishing on Thompson Creek. As she told the story, a big grin came over her face. "Few things have thrilled me as much as learning to fish. Sitting on the creek banks and feeling the tug on the line and pulling out a perky perch was so much fun. Then later, PawPaw fried up those fish in that old black pot. Now that was the best."

CRAB AU GRATIN

1 pound lump crab-
   meat
1 cup finely chopped
   onion
1/2 cup finely
   chopped celery
1/4 cup finely
   chopped bell
   pepper
6 Tablespoons butter
4 Tablespoons all-
   purpose flour
1 (12-ounce) can
   evaporated milk
2 teaspoons
   Worcestershire
   sauce
1 egg yolk (beaten)
1 teaspoon salt
1/4 teaspoon black
   pepper
1/4 teaspoon red
   pepper
1/4 pound grated
   Cheddar cheese

Sauté onion, celery, and bell pepper in butter until barely tender.

Blend flour into vegetables. Combine milk, Worcestershire sauce,
egg yolk, and seasonings in a separate bowl. Whisk to blend. Pour
into vegetable mixture. Simmer
over medium heat 3 minutes.
Remove from heat. Fold in crabmeat. Pour into a greased 2-quart
casserole dish. Sprinkle with grated cheese.

Bake at 350 degrees - 20-25 minutes.

SHRIMP STUFFED PASTA ROLLS

(w/cheese sauce)

STUFFING

8 (4-inch) pasta tubes
1 (10-ounce) box frozen spinach (thawed)
1/2 pound ground beef
1 Tablespoon olive oil
1/3 cup finely chopped onion
2 teaspoons minced garlic
1 (8-ounce) can corn
2 Tablespoons all-purpose flour
2/3 cup beef broth
1 pound shrimp (peeled & deveined)
1/3 cup chopped black olives
1/2 teaspoon salt
1/4 teaspoon pepper

SAUCE

3 Tablespoons butter
2 Tablespoons all-purpose flour
1 cup half & half
2/3 cup Parmesan cheese
1/4 teaspoon white pepper

Cook pasta according to package directions. Drain and rinse in cool water. Layer in bottom of casserole dish.

Cook spinach in boiling water 4 minutes. Drain and set aside

Heat oil in a large skillet. Add meat, onion, garlic, and corn to hot oil. Cook over medium heat until meat is browned (approximately 5-6 minutes).

Heat beef broth to lukewarm. Combine with flour to make a thin paste. Pour over meat and vegetables. Add shrimp, olives, and seasonings. Simmer 5-6 minutes.

Let mixture cool slightly. Stuff pasta with mixture. Arrange in casserole dish. Make a layer of drained spinach over shells.

Melt butter until sizzling. Stir in flour. Blend thoroughly. Gradually stir in half & half, cheese, and pepper. Pour sauce over spinach.

Bake at 350 degrees - 30 minutes.

SHRIMP, CHICKEN, AND SAUSAGE FAVORITE

3/4 cup chopped mushrooms

3/4 cup finely chopped onion

1/2 cup finely chopped green onion

1/3 cup finely chopped bell pepper

2 cloves garlic (minced)

3 Tablespoons butter

3 cups cooked chicken

1 pound smoked sausage (cut into 1/2-inch slices)

2 (8-ounce) cans tomato sauce

1 (10-ounce) can chopped Rotel tomatoes

1 cup water

1 (4-ounce) can black olives

1 pound shrimp

Sauté mushrooms, onions, bell pepper, and garlic in butter in a large pot. Add remaining ingredients, except olives and shrimp. Cover. Simmer 25 minutes. Add olives and shrimp. Simmer additional 15 minutes.

Serve over rice.

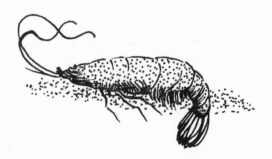

SHRIMP AND SAUSAGE SPAGHETTI

12 ounces spaghetti
1 Tablespoon butter
2 pounds shrimp
1 Tablespoon freshly
    squeezed lemon
    juice
1 teaspoon paprika
2 Tablespoons olive oil
1-1/2 pounds smoked
    sausage (cut into
    1/4-inch slices)
1/2 cup finely chopped
    onion
1/2 cup finely chopped
    green onion
2 cloves garlic
    (minced)
1 (14.5-ounce) can
    chopped tomatoes
1 (10-ounce) can Rotel
    tomatoes
1 Tablespoon tomato
    paste
1 package spaghetti
    mix
1 teaspoon sugar
1/2 teaspoon oregano
1/2 teaspoon sweet
    basil
1/2 teaspoon salt
1/4 teaspoon pepper
1/2 cup fresh finely
    chopped parsley

Cook spaghetti according to package directions. Drain and toss in butter. Set aside.

Squeeze lemon juice over shrimp. Sprinkle with paprika.

Heat olive oil in a large skillet or Dutch oven. Brown sausage, onions, and garlic in hot oil. Drain excess oil. Add tomatoes, tomato paste, spaghetti mix, sugar, and seasonings to mixture. Cover and simmer 15 minutes.

Add shrimp and parsley. Leave uncovered. Simmer 6-7 minutes or until shrimp turn pink.

PAN-FRIED LOUISIANA CATFISH
(w/shrimp sauce)

SAUCE

1/4 cup margarine
3 Tablespoons
  all-purpose flour
1/2 teaspoon salt
1/4 teaspoon white
  pepper
1 cup milk
1 cup chopped cooked
  shrimp

Melt margarine until bubbly. Stir in flour until blended. Add seasonings. Gradually add milk. Cook over medium heat until mixture thickens. Add shrimp and heat thoroughly. Cover to keep sauce warm while preparing fish.

PAN FRIED FISH

2-1/2 pounds catfish
  fillets
3 slices bacon
4 Tablespoons butter
1 cup all-purpose flour
1 teaspoon salt
1/2 teaspoon pepper
1/8 teaspoon baking
  powder

Wash and pat dry fish fillets.

Fry bacon in a large skillet until crisp. Remove bacon from grease and set aside. Melt butter in skillet with grease.

Combine flour with remaining ingredients. Dredge fish in flour mixture. Pan fry fish in hot grease and butter mixture until thoroughly cooked and browned. Using a slotted spoon, remove from grease to buttered platter. Crumble bacon over fish. Pour sauce over fish.

TANGY BAKED CATFISH

2 pounds catfish fillets
  (3/4-inch thickness)
1 teaspoon salt
4 Tablespoons butter
1/4 cup lemon juice
2 Tablespoons white
  wine
2 teaspoons
  Worcestershire
  sauce
1 Tablespoon dried
  parsley
2 teaspoons lemon
  pepper
1/4 teaspoon sweet
  basil
1/4 teaspoon red
  pepper
1/4 cup grated
  Parmesan cheese

Rinse fillets with cool water. Pat dry. Sprinkle with salt. Fish must be thoroughly dried. Set aside.

In a small saucepan, melt butter. Add lemon juice, wine, Worcestershire sauce, parsley, lemon pepper, basil, and red pepper. Bring to a rolling boil. Remove from heat. Allow sauce to cool. Lay fillets in a foil lined pan coated with vegetable spray. Spoon sauce over fish. Cover loosely with foil. Bake on bottom rack of oven. (Baste at least one time while baking.)

Bake at 325 degrees - 12-15 minutes or until fish is flaky.

Uncover, baste, and move to top rack. Sprinkle with cheese.

Broil at 450 degrees until lightly browned and crusty around edges.

Fish will be very tangy immediately after baking, but will become more mellow if allowed to set for a while.

BAKED CATFISH

2 pounds catfish fillets
3 Tablespoons lime
   juice
1 teaspoon salt
4 Tablespoons butter
1/2 cup mild Cheddar
   cheese
1/2 cup milk
1/4 cup white wine
1 teaspoon white
   pepper
1/4 teaspoon garlic
   powder
1/4 teaspoon onion
   powder
1/8 teaspoon cayenne
   pepper
1/8 teaspoon nutmeg
1/2 cup plain bread
   crumbs
4 slices bacon (cooked
   & crumbled)

Wash fish and pat thoroughly dry. Using a pastry brush, coat fish with lime juice. Sprinkle with 1/2 teaspoon salt. Place fillets in a greased casserole dish.

In a saucepan, combine butter, cheese, milk, wine, remaining seasonings, and nutmeg. Heat thoroughly. Cool mixture several minutes. Pour over fish.

Cover with breadcrumbs and bacon. Leave uncovered.

Bake at 350 - 40-45 minutes.

PAN-FRIED CATFISH CAKES

1 pound catfish fillets
2 Tablespoons lemon
   juice
1 teaspoon Creole
   seasoning
2 Tablespoons butter
1/2 cup finely chopped
   onion
1 Tablespoon finely
   chopped jalapeno
   pepper
1/4 cup mayonnaise
2 teaspoons mustard
2 teaspoons
   Worcestershire sauce
1 teaspoon sugar
1/2 teaspoon salt
1/4 teaspoon black
   pepper
1/4 teaspoon garlic
   powder
1/8 teaspoon cayenne
   pepper
1 Tablespoon dried
   parsley
1 egg (beaten)
1-1/4 cups seasoned
   breadcrumbs

Wash and pat dry fish. Place in shallow greased baking dish. Drizzle lemon juice over fish. Sprinkle with Creole seasoning. Cover with aluminum foil.

Bake at 350 degrees - 20 minutes or until fish is flaky.

Sauté onion in butter until transparent. Add flaked fish. Combine remaining ingredients and mix thoroughly. Shape into 3-inch patties. Refrigerate 30 minutes.

Using only enough oil to cover bottom of a 10-inch skillet, pan fry until patties are lightly browned on both sides. Turn fish patties only once while cooking.

Fishing along the banks of rivers and bayous is not a rare sight in the South today. Many of those fishing in early spring sit atop a tin bucket with a handcut cane pole.

SEAFOOD, SAUSAGE, AND CHICKEN GUMBO

1 large fryer (cut into serving-size pieces)

2 Tablespoons Creole seasoning (divided)

2 pounds shrimp (peeled & deveined)

2 (6-ounce) cans crab meat

1 pound smoked sausage (cut into 1/4-inch wafers)

4 quarts water

1 pint Savoie Roux

1 large white onion (finely chopped)

1 bunch green onions (finely chopped)

1 large green bell pepper (finely chopped)

3 stalks celery (finely chopped)

3 cloves garlic (minced)

1 teaspoon salt

1/2 teaspoon red pepper

1/2 teaspoon garlic powder

In a large bowl, sprinkle chicken with 2 teaspoons Creole seasoning. Cover with plastic wrap and refrigerate at least 1 hour. In a separate medium glass bowl, combine crab meat and shrimp. Season with 2 teaspoons Creole seasoning. Cover with plastic wrap and refrigerate at least 1 hour.

In a heavy 10-quart pot, heat water to rapid boil. Add roux, 1 heaping Tablespoon at a time, into boiling water. Stir constantly with wooden spoon until each addition is dissolved. (Make certain that roux does not stick to bottom of pot.) Add vegetables to boiling mixture. Reduce heat to medium for 20 minutes. (Do not cover gumbo at any time while cooking.)

Heat oil until sizzling in a large iron skillet. Add chicken pieces and lightly brown (no more than 6-7 minutes total browning time.) Add chicken and all drippings from skillet to liquid. Add 2 teaspoons Creole seasoning, salt, pepper, and garlic powder. Leave uncovered and simmer 1 hour. Add sausage and simmer 15 minutes. Add shrimp and crab meat and simmer additional 20 minutes.

Filé may be used to enhance the flavor of gumbo. A pint of oysters with liquid may be added with shrimp and crab meat. (Oysters are said to be best in those months with (r's) in them.)

SHRIMP STEW

1 pound medium shrimp (peeled & deveined)

2 teaspoons paprika

3 Tablespoons all-purpose flour

3 Tablespoons cooking oil

1/2 pound smoked sausage (cut into 1/2-inch pieces)

3/4 cup finely chopped onion

1/2 cup finely chopped celery

1/2 cup finely chopped green pepper

3 cloves garlic (minced)

1 (10-1/2 ounce) can chicken broth

1/4 cup clam juice

2 (14.5-ounce) cans stewed tomatoes w/juice

1/2 cup water

2 teaspoons Creole seasoning

Sprinkle paprika over shrimp. Set aside

Combine oil and flour. Cook over high heat, stirring constantly until mixture turns golden brown.

Add sausage and vegetables to hot roux. Cook over medium heat 5 minutes. Add remaining ingredients and bring mixture to a rolling boil. Cover. Simmer 15 minutes. Add shrimp. Cover. Simmer additional 7 minutes.

Serve over hot rice.

FISH STEW

3-4 pounds catfish
  steaks
1 Tablespoon lemon
  juice
1 cup finely chopped
  onion
1/4 cup finely
  chopped green
  onion
1/3 cup finely
  chopped parsley
1 (8-ounce) can
  tomato sauce
1/4 cup vegetable oil
2 Tablespoons all-
  purpose flour
2 teaspoons Creole
  seasoning

Wash and pat dry fish. Sprinkle with lemon juice.

In a large cast iron pot, make a layer of onions and parsley. Lay fish over vegetables.

In a small bowl, combine remaining ingredients. Whisk to blend thoroughly. Pour over fish. Cover and simmer 1 hour. (Do not stir stew. To prevent sticking, hold pot by handle and gently shake 2-3 times while stew is cooking.) Add a small amount of water to stew if needed for additional gravy.

The murky rivers and bayous that thread the southern landscape have rendered a significant source of sustenance for generations. That old black pot, sizzling with hot grease, was kept ready to "brown-up" a "mess" of perch or catfish. Even today, rare is the Southerner who will turn down cornmeal-dredged fried fish.

OYSTER STEW

2 pints oysters
1 teaspoon Creole
  seasoning
1 teaspoon paprika
4 Tablespoons butter
1/2 cup finely
  chopped onion
1/4 cup finely
  chopped green
  onion
1 cup thinly sliced
  fresh mushrooms
3 Tablespoons flour
1 teaspoon salt
1/4 teaspoon black
  pepper
1/4 teaspoon red
  pepper
1 cup half & half
2 cups milk
1 cup grated Cheddar
  cheese
1 (10-1/2-ounce) can
  cream of potato
  soup
1 teaspoon hot sauce
1 Tablespoon dried
  parsley

Sprinkle drained oysters with Creole seasoning and paprika.

Sauté onions in butter until tender. Stir in mushrooms and sauté 2 minutes. Stir in flour and seasonings. Reduce heat and gradually pour milk into mixture. Stir constantly until mixture thickens. Add cheese, soup, hot sauce, and oysters. Simmer until oysters begin to curl on edges. Garnish with parsley.

FISH AND SEAFOOD SAUCES

FISH SAUCE - Grate 1 small unpeeled cucumber. (Remove any outside waxy residue by washing thoroughly.) Lay on paper towels and sprinkle with 1/4 teaspoon salt. Let set 1 hour. Press to remove any excess liquid. Whip 1/2 cup whipping cream until stiff. Stir in grated cucumber, 1/8 teaspoon white pepper, and 1 Tablespoon lime juice. (1/4 teaspoon dill weed may be added.)

SEAFOOD SAUCE - Combine 1/2 cup barbecue sauce, 1/3 cup catsup, 1 teaspoon Worcestershire sauce, 1/2 teaspoon garlic powder, 1/3 cup finely chopped onion, 1/3 cup finely chopped celery. Combine all ingredients. Mix thoroughly. Chill several hours.

COCKTAIL SAUCE - Combine the following ingredients. 3/4 cup catsup, 1/2 cup sherry, 1 Tablespoon apple cider vinegar, 1 Tablespoon Worcestershire sauce, 1 Tablespoon creamy horseradish, 1 Tablespoon grated onion, 1 Tablespoon finely chopped green pepper, 1 teaspoon sugar, and 1 teaspoon Creole seasoning. Mix well. Chill several hours.

TARTAR SAUCE - Combine 1 cup mayonnaise, 1/2 cup sour cream, 2 Tablespoons sweet pickle relish, 2 Tablespoons grated onion, 2 Tablespoons finely chopped green onion, 2 Tablespoons finely chopped fresh parsley, and 2 Tablespoons lemon juice. Mix thoroughly.

HOLLANDAISE SAUCE - In a double boiler, combine 3 egg yolks, 1/4 teaspoon salt, 1/8 teaspoon white pepper, and 1/8 teaspoon cayenne pepper. Beat to mix. Gradually add 2 Tablespoons lemon juice. Cook over medium heat. Add 1/3 cup butter, 1 Tablespoon at a time. Stir constantly to melt butter. Sauce will thicken while cooking.

wild game
outdoor cooking

*W*e were up before daybreak, but not before Mama. The spicy aroma of frying chicken, along with breakfast bacon, perfumed the air. By the time we dressed and wolfed breakfast, Momma had lunch packed and Pa had the truck loaded. Grandpa, Uncle Bud, and Pa rode in the cab while all us kids and the women rode in the truck bed. One of the littler ones would jump out to open the gates as we made our way through the woods to the Honey Hole on Hurricane Creek. Pa would balance the truck between the ruts, and everyone but Pa would bail out and push whenever we got stuck. Mama supervised.

Once on the creek bank, we baited up and played the shallows for brim beds. Blue gills and sun perch would suck the cork under with a pop, and squeals of delight would spill from the children. The older men cast across the creek, fishing for large mouth bass. They would walk down the creek and cross from side to side over logs. Every now and then, we could hear Uncle Bud slip and fall in. Grandpa cut a set pole, baited up for catfish, and settled against a pin oak for his morning nap. Mama, Grandma, and Aunt Suzie helped us kids bait up, retrieve hangups, and unsnarl line.

By noon, all the food was usually gone, Uncle Bud was wet, and Pa was back with a fine stringer. We'd load up the washtub of brim and Pa's bass and head for home.

wild game and outdoor cooking

MUSCADINE WILD TURKEY

1 whole wild turkey

1 cup muscadine
  sauce

1 stick margarine
  (softened)

2 Tablespoons Creole
  seasoning

2 teaspoons onion salt

2 teaspoons garlic
  powder

1/2 cup Worcestershire
  sauce

1/4 cup mustard

1 medium apple
  (coarsely chopped
  w/peel)

1 medium orange
  (sliced with peel)

6 slices bacon

Use hand to loosen area between skin and meaty part of turkey.

Prepare a sauce from next 7 ingredients. Rub mixture under skin of turkey and over surface.

Stuff cavity of bird with apple and orange. Place strips of bacon over top of turkey. Cook in charcoal smoker over medium heat 5-6 hours. (Cooking time may vary depending on size of turkey.)

Use a meat thermometer to determine doneness.

Hunting and fishing have always been favored sports in the Rural South, but during the hard years, sport was not the prime motivation. The "menfolk" needed to be skilled in the woods to fulfill their role as provider for the family. Nature's bountiful wild harvest was an important food source that was not to be wasted.

DUTCH OVEN
WILD TURKEY BREAST

1 turkey breast
1-1/2 teaspoons lemon
pepper
1 teaspoon salt
5 Tablespoons oil
1 (12-ounce) can
frozen orange juice
concentrate
1-1/4 cups water
3 Tablespoons brown
sugar
1 teaspoon cinnamon
1 teaspoon ground
cloves
1 teaspoon celery
powder
1/2 teaspoon garlic
powder
1/2 teaspoon curry
powder
1 (8-ounce) can
pineapple chunks
(drained)
1/4 cup raisins
3 Tablespoons
cornstarch

Rub turkey breast with lemon pepper and salt. Heat oil in Dutch oven. Brown turkey breast in hot oil.

Combine orange juice, 1/2 cup water, brown sugar, spices and seasonings. Heat thoroughly. Whisk to blend. Pour mixture over turkey. Add pineapple and raisins to pot. Bring to a rolling boil. Cover and simmer over medium heat 2 hours. Remove turkey from pot.

Combine remaining 3/4 cup of water with cornstarch. Blend well. Stir into juice mixture. Cook over medium heat until liquid becomes slightly thickened. Return breast to pot. Baste with liquid.

DUTCH OVEN DUCKS

3 large ducks
1-1/2 cups butter
  (softened)
1 Tablespoon Creole
  seasoning
1 teaspoon celery
  salt
1 teaspoon sage
2 small onions
  (chopped)
1 large bell pepper
  (chopped)
5 cloves garlic
  (minced)
1/4 cup finely
  chopped jalapeño
  peppers
2 small apples
  (cored &
  quartered)
3/4 cup water

Combine butter and seasonings to make a paste. Rub over surface and under skin of ducks.

Combine chopped vegetables and apples. Stuff into cavity of ducks. Place ducks in a large Dutch oven. Add water. Cover with tight fitting lid. Cook over medium heat 1 hour. Uncover and simmer 25 minutes.

Additional water may be added.

GRILL ROASTED DUCK

4 wild ducks
1 teaspoon salt
1 teaspoon pepper
1/2 teaspoon thyme
1/2 teaspoon sage
3/4 cup butter (melted)
8 slices bacon
(cut in half)

Wash ducks and pat dry. Combine seasonings. Rub over surface of ducks. Baste ducks with melted butter. Stuff each cavity with dressing. Place 2 strips of bacon on foil. Arrange duck over bacon. Place 2 bacon strips over ducks. Wrap foil tightly around each bird. Grill over medium heat 1 hour. Turn twice during grilling time. Remove ducks from fire. Open top of foil. Return to grill for 25-30 additional minutes.

RICE DRESSING
1 cup wild rice
2 cups chicken broth
1/2 teaspoon salt
1 teaspoon garlic
powder
1 stick butter
3/4 cup chopped
mushrooms
1/2 cup finely chopped
celery
2 whole green onions
(finely chopped)
2 Tablespoons finely
chopped green
pepper
1/2 cup finely chopped
pecans (toasted)
1/2 cup tomato sauce

Wash rice. In a medium saucepan, combine broth, salt, and garlic powder. Bring liquid to a rolling boil. Stir in rice. Cover and simmer until rice is tender.

Melt butter in a skillet. Sauté vegetables until tender. Add pecans, rice, and tomato sauce. Mix well.

SKILLET QUAIL

6-8 quail
2 cups milk
2 teaspoons salt
1 teaspoon pepper
1 teaspoon paprika
1/8 teaspoon cayenne
1 cup all-purpose
  flour
1/3 cup shortening
1 stick butter
1 bunch green onions
  (finely chopped)
1/4 cup finely
  chopped green
  pepper
4 cloves minced
  garlic
1 Tablespoon roux
  and gravy mix
2 (4-ounce) cans
  mushrooms and
  liquid
1/2 cup cooking
  sherry
1 cup water

Cut each quail in half. Soak in milk for 30 minutes. Combine seasonings in a separate bowl. Drain quail. Sprinkle with seasonings. Dredge in flour. Lightly brown quail in hot oil. Remove quail and set aside.

In a separate skillet, sauté onions, green pepper, and garlic in butter until vegetables are lightly browned.

In the skillet with drippings, reheat oil and stir in roux mix. Add mushrooms. Return quail and sauteéd vegetables to skillet. Add sherry and 1/2 cup water. Cover and simmer 30-40 minutes. Add remaining water and simmer 15-20 additional minutes.

QUAIL WITH WINE

8 quail
1 Tablespoon Creole seasoning
1-1/2 cups red wine
2/3 cup orange juice
1 cup chopped dried apples
3 cloves
1 cup cooked rice
1 teaspoon grated orange peel
1/2 teaspoon ginger
1/2 cup butter (melted)
1 cup chopped walnuts

Wash and pat dry quail. Rub seasoning in cavity and over surface of each quail.

Combine wine, orange juice, apple pieces, and cloves in a saucepan. Bring to a boil. Reduce heat and simmer 10 minutes. Remove cloves.

In a mixing bowl, combine 2/3 cup wine mixture with remaining ingredients. Stuff each quail with rice mixture. Cover the bottom of a shallow roasting pan with water. Place quail on a rack in pan. Cover loosely with foil.

Bake at 425 degrees - 5 minutes. Reduce heat to 325 degrees 25 minutes. Remove foil last 10 minutes.

Baste frequently with remaining wine mixture.

OUTDOOR DUTCH OVEN VENISON ROAST

4-5 pound venison roast

2 medium onions (sliced into rings)

1/2 cup cooking oil

1 (10-3/4-ounce) can cream of mushroom soup

1 (14.5-ounce) can chicken broth

1 teaspoon salt

3 Tablespoons mustard

2 Tablespoons Worcestershire sauce

1 Tablespoon garlic powder

2 teaspoons pepper

1 teaspoon Creole seasoning

6 medium potatoes (peeled & cubed)

Light charcoal and let burn until a light gray ash covers the coals. Place 8 - 10 pieces of charcoal on the ground in a circle (size of Dutch oven). Place oven on coals. Coals may be added or removed as needed to regulate heat.

Brown onions and roast in a large Dutch oven 10-12 minutes.

Combine remaining ingredients, except potatoes, in a large mixing bowl. Whisk to blend. Pour mixture over roast and onions. Cover. Place 8-10 coals over the top of pot.

Simmer 2-1/2 - 3 hours or until roast is tender. (Water may be added as needed.) Add potatoes and simmer additional 30-45 minutes.

PINEY WOODS VENISON ROAST

3 pound venison roast
1 teaspoon salt
1 teaspoon garlic
   powder
1 teaspoon celery
   powder
1 teaspoon thyme
6 whole cloves
1 bay leaf
4 cups water
3 medium potatoes
   (quartered)
2 medium onions
   (peeled &
   quartered)
2 celery stalks (cut
   into 1-inch pieces)
1 teaspoon Creole
   instant roux and
   gravy mix

Combine seasonings. Rub over surface of roast. Stuff cloves into roast. Lower meat into water. Heat to boiling. Drop bay leaf into water. Cover and simmer 2 hours.

Add vegetables and simmer until tender. Remove roast from broth. Remove cloves and bay leaf. Add roux mix to make gravy.

Turnips my be substituted for potatoes.

RUMP OF VENISON STEAKS

6-8 pound venison steaks (cut into 2-3-inch thickness)

1 Tablespoon Creole seasoning

3 cups apple cider vinegar

1 cup white wine

1/4 cup honey

1/4 cup soy sauce

3 Tablespoons spiced mustard

3 Tablespoons brown sugar

1 Tablespoon cornstarch

Rub steaks with seasoning. Set aside.

Combine remaining ingredients, except cornstarch, in a Dutch oven. Whisk to blend. Add steaks to liquid. Cover and cook over medium-low heat 1 hour. Remove meat from liquid. Add cornstarch to liquid. Cook on medium heat until mixture thickens.

Arrange steaks on grill away from direct heat. Baste with glaze at 15 minute intervals. Smoke approximately 1 hour. Remove meat and slice into 1/2 - 1/4-inch strips.

Hickory, cherry, or pecan chips may be added to fire for additional flavor

ELK CHOPS SUPREME

6 loin chops (3/4-inch thickness)
1 cup Italian salad dressing
1 cup soy sauce
1/2 cup sherry
1/2 cup brown sugar
1 Tablespoon garlic salt
1 Tablespoon onion powder
1 Tablespoon celery powder
2 teaspoons cinnamon
1 teaspoon pepper

Place chops in a large glass dish. In a small bowl, combine remaining ingredients. Whisk to blend thoroughly. Marinate overnight. Drain chops. Place on hot grill approximately 5 inches above charcoal fire. Turn frequently while cooking. Baste with marinade. (Approximately 30-35 minutes cooking time.)

STUFFED MOOSE STEAKS

4-6 moose steaks
(cut 1-1/2 inches in
thickness)

1 cup garlic croutons

1/2 cup grated
Cheddar cheese

2 Tablespoons
currants

3 Tablespoons
margarine (melted)

2 Tablespoons orange
juice

1 Tablespoon lemon
pepper

1/4 teaspoon salt

1/8 teaspoon
cinnamon

Cut small pockets in all sides of steaks.

Combine croutons, cheese, and currants. In a separate bowl, combine margarine, orange juice and seasonings. Mix well. Pour over croutons and toss to mix. Stuff pockets with crouton stuffing. Place steaks over medium-hot charcoals. Grill approximately 30-40 minutes.

BASTING SAUCE

1 cup Italian salad
dressing

1/2 cup Worcestershire
sauce

2 Tablespoons soy
sauce

Combine ingredients and whisk to blend. Baste meat at 10 minute intervals while cooking.

WILD PORK POT

2-1/2 pounds loin
   chops
1 teaspoon paprika
5 Tablespoons oil
1/4 cup water
1/2 cup finely chopped
   onion
1/2 cup finely chopped
   green pepper
4 cloves garlic (minced)
1 (14.5-ounce) can
   chicken broth
1 (14.5-ounce) can
   stewed tomatoes
2 Tablespoons soy
   sauce
1 teaspoon salt
1/4 teaspoon pepper
1 cup rice
1/4 cup chopped
   pimientos

Sprinkle loin chops with paprika. In a Dutch oven, brown pork in hot oil. Pour water into pot. Layer onion, green pepper, and garlic over pork. Cover and cook until vegetables are soft.

Pour broth, tomatoes, and soy sauce over pork and vegetables. Season with salt and pepper. Bring mixture to a boil. Stir in rice. Cover and cook over medium heat 40-45 minutes. Add pimientos while lightly fluffing rice.

CAMP HOUSE RABBIT

2 rabbits (cut into
  serving-size pieces)
1 teaspoon salt
1 teaspoon white
  pepper
8 slices bacon (cut
  into 2-inch squares)
1-1/2 cups flour
1 cup finely chopped
  onion
8 large mushrooms
  (quartered)
1-1/2 cups beef broth
1 cup sour cream

Season meat with salt and pepper. Set aside. Cook bacon in a large Dutch oven until crisp. Remove bacon from pot. Leave drippings to brown meat. Dredge rabbit in flour to coat. Brown rabbit on all sides.

Add onion, mushrooms, and broth. Cover and cook over medium heat 25-30 minutes or until meat is well done. Remove rabbit from the pot. Add sour cream to liquid in pot. Whisk to blend. Heat thoroughly. Pour over rabbit. Crumble bacon over meat.

Serve over wild rice.

SMOKED FISH

3-4 pounds fish fillets
8/10 slices bacon

Wash and pat dry fish fillets.

In a covered grill or smoker, start a charcoal fire at one end of the grill. Use hickory or sassafras chips on glowing embers. Place a sheet of heavy aluminum foil away from the direct source of heat. Place bacon slices on foil.

MARINADE
1/2 cup brown sugar
2 Tablespoons minced garlic
2 cups water
2 cups apple cider
1-1/2 cups Italian dressing
1 cup Worcestershire sauce
1/4 cup soy sauce
3 Tablespoons salt
2 Tablespoons Creole seasoning
1 Tablespoon onion powder
1 Tablespoon celery powder

Combine brown sugar, garlic, liquid ingredients, and seasonings in a large mixing bowl. Whisk to blend. Pour marinade over fillets. Refrigerate at least 4 hours. Turn fish every hour.

Place fillets on bacon leaving space between each piece. Close lid of grill or smoker. Smoke approximately 4 hours. Smoking time varies depending on heat and thickness of fillets. Open grill only to baste. Do not turn fish. Maintain medium heat while cooking. Fillets will cook to a dark honey-brown color.

Catfish, bass, redfish, or crappie may be used.

CAMPERS DUTCH OVEN BISCUITS AND GRAVY

BISCUITS
1-1/4 cups all-purpose flour
1 teaspoon baking powder
1/4 teaspoon salt
3 Tablespoons shortening
1/4 teaspoon baking soda
1/2 cup buttermilk

Prepare 12-14 glowing coals to cook biscuits. Place 5-6 under the Dutch oven. Temperature should be approximately 500 degrees.

Melt 1 Tablespoon shortening in Dutch oven. Spread over bottom and sides approximately 2-1/2 inches up sides. Combine flour, baking powder, and salt. Mix well. Cut in 2 Tablespoons shortening. Add soda to buttermilk and let set 5 minutes. Add flour to buttermilk. Mix to form a soft dough. Turn out on a floured surface. Knead 8-10 times. Pinch off sections of dough approximately 2-inch balls. Roll out between hands to 1-2-inch thickness. Roll each biscuit in melted shortening to coat both sides. Arrange from center out in Dutch oven with each biscuit touching.

Bake at 500 degrees - 10-12 minutes.

GRAVY
1/2 pound hot
  ground sausage
2 Tablespoons
  all-purpose flour
2 cups warm milk

Brown sausage. Pour off excess grease, reserving at least 2 Tablespoons. Stir in flour. Gradually add milk, stirring con- stantly. Cook until liquid thickens.

Big Mama's Tips For Sweets and Treats

Pies

The pastry covering a pie will brown more evenly if brushed with melted butter or a beaten egg white. Sprinkle with sugar to give an old-fashioned look.

To test for doneness of a custard filling, insert a knife one inch from the center. The pie will be done when the knife comes out clean. Doneness may also be checked by lightly pressing the top of a pie with the index finger. The pie will be ready when the center area (one inch or smaller) is firm to a light touch. Take care to avoid overcooking custards.

For meringue, separate eggs while cold, but let set to room temperature before beating. Use a small teaspoon to remove all specks of yolks from whites. Use a glass or metal bowl for whipping egg whites.

Meringue should be spread to the edge of the crust to seal and prevent

*meringue from shrinking
away from the pie edges.*

*Coat a knife with butter
before slicing the pie and
then dip in water after
cutting each piece.*

*When using a com-
mercial whipped topping,
blend in two tablespoons
of powdered sugar to
keep the topping firm.*

Cakes

*All ingredients should be
at room temperature.*

*Butter and sugar should
be creamed until the
grainy texture is gone.*

*Add dry ingredients in
three portions, beginning
and ending with dry
ingredients.*

*Bake a cake on the
center rack in an oven.*

*After removing a cake
from the oven, leave in
the pan for ten minutes.
Remove and let the cake
cool on a wire baking
rack.*

Cookies

*All ingredients should be
at room temperature.*

*Use an electric mixer to
cream sugar, butter, and
eggs. Blend all other
ingredients by hand.
Cookie dough that is
over-worked will have a
cake-like texture.*

*Do not grease the cookie
sheet before baking.*

*After baking a batch of
cookies, the baking sheet
should be cooled
thoroughly before using
again. The sheet should
have a clean surface.*

*Bake only one sheet of
cookies at a time on the
middle rack of the oven.*

*Do not over-bake
cookies. For soft, chewy
texture, remove cookies
from the oven as soon as
the edges begin to brown.
Leave on the baking
sheet four to five minutes.
At this stage, the cookies
will appear to be under-
baked, but after cooling
on a wire rack, the
cookies should be
perfectly baked.*

pies and desserts

big mama's caramel sugar cream pie, *198*

peanut butter cream cheese pie, *199*

french silk chocolate pie, *200*

lem's chocolate chip pie, *201*

lemon chess pie, *202*

lemon meringue pie w/homemade pie crust, *203*

coconut pie, *204*

sweet potato pie, *205*

pecan pie, *206*

cheesecake pecan pie, *207*

apple cobbler, *208*

blueberry pie, *209*

easy peach pie, *210*

fruit pie, *211*

bread pudding w/vanilla-rum sauce, *212*

caramel-toffee ice cream dessert, *213*

cheesecake wesley, *214*

chocolate eclair dessert, *215*

peach crisp surprise, *216*

nana's strawberry shortcake, *217*

dessert toppings, *218*

BIG MAMA'S CARAMEL SUGAR CREAM PIE

1 (9-inch) pie crust (baked)

3/4 cup sugar

4 Tablespoons cornstarch

2 cups whipping cream

10 caramel candy pieces

6 Tablespoons butter (cut into large pieces)

1/2 teaspoon vanilla extract

3/4 teaspoon nutmeg

Sift sugar and cornstarch together in a heavy saucepan. Gradually stir in cream. Whisk to blend mixture. Cook over medium heat, stirring constantly, until mixture thickens. Remove from heat and add caramel candy, butter, and vanilla. Whisk mixture until caramels and butter are melted. Pour filling into baked pie crust. Sprinkle with nutmeg.

Bake at 350 degrees - 12-15 minutes.

*Options for entertainment were limited to the creative imagination. An opportunity to play came as a welcome relief from the boredom of daily farm chores. Red rover, leap frog, hop scotch, marbles, and jump rope were some of the after-supper games of choice. Talk to any real Southerner who grew up in "the good old days," and there are always delightful stories about "fun," "treats," and "sweets." The last section of **Big Mama's Back in the Kitchen** is dedicated to childhood memories and sweet things to eat.*

PEANUT BUTTER CREAM CHEESE PIE

CRUST

1 cup graham cracker crumbs

1/4 cup butter (melted)

1/4 cup brown sugar

Combine ingredients. Press mixture into 9-inch pan to form crust. Chill until ready to use.

FILLING

1-1/3 cups peanut butter

2 cups sugar

2 Tablespoons butter (melted)

2 teaspoons vanilla

2 (8-ounce) packages cream cheese

1-1/2 cups heavy whipping cream

Combine peanut butter, sugar, butter, vanilla, and cream cheese. In a second bowl, beat whipping cream until cream forms peaks and is very fluffy. Blend cream into peanut butter mixture by hand. Whip until all mixture is an even brown color. Pour into pie crust. Chill at least 6 hours.

TOPPING

3 (1.55 ounce) chocolate candy bars

Melt candy over low heat. Drizzle over chilled pie.

FRENCH SILK CHOCOLATE PIE

1 9-inch pastry shell (baked)

1 cup whipping cream

1 (6-ounce) package semi-sweet chocolate pieces

1/2 cup butter

1/2 cup sugar

3 egg yolks

3 Tablespoons milk

1 teaspoon vanilla extract

1/8 teaspoon almond extract

1 (8-ounce) carton frozen whipped topping (partially thawed)

3 Tablespoons powdered sugar

1 (2-ounce) Butterfinger candy bar (crushed)

Combine whipping cream, chocolate pieces, butter, and sugar in a large heavy saucepan. Cook over low heat, stirring constantly, until chocolate is melted. Remove 1/2 of chocolate from pot to a small bowl. Gradually add beaten egg yolks to mixture, beating after each addition. Return egg mixture to pot. Cook over medium-low heat until filling begins to thicken (approximately 4-5 minutes).

Remove from heat. Add milk and extracts to mixture. Beat only to blend thoroughly. Set mixture in a large bowl filled with water and ice cubes. Whip at intervals until mixture begins to become firm (approximately 15 minutes). Remove from water and beat 4-5 minutes on high speed until mixture becomes fluffy. Spoon filling into baked pie crust. Refrigerate several hours.

Just before serving, combine topping and powdered sugar. Beat only until mixture is smooth. Add dollops to pie. Sprinkle with crushed candy bar.

LEM'S CHOCOLATE CHIP PIE

1 (9-inch) deep dish pie crust (baked)
1 cup sugar
1/3 cup butter
3/4 cup light corn syrup
2 Tablespoons flour
3 eggs (beaten)
2 teaspoons vanilla extract
1/4 teaspoon salt
1 cup semi-sweet chocolate pieces
3/4 cup coarsely chopped pecans (toasted)

Combine sugar and butter. Beat until creamy. Add corn syrup, flour, eggs, vanilla, and salt. Beat until well blended. Sprinkle chocolate pieces and pecans over bottom of pastry shell. Pour filling over mixture.

Bake at 325 degrees - 45 minutes.

Do you remember swinging from vines that hung over high bluffs or swinging in that old tire swing?

LEMON CHESS PIE

1 (9-inch) pie crust
2 cups sugar
2 Tablespoons flour
2 Tablespoons
cornmeal
4 eggs (beaten)
1/4 cup melted butter
1/4 cup milk
1/4 cup lemon juice
1 Tablespoon grated
lemon rind

Bake pie crust at 400 degrees 7-8 minutes. Let cool.

Combine dry ingredients. Add eggs, one at a time, beating after each addition. Add remaining ingredients. Beat to blend. Pour mixture into partially baked pie crust.

Bake at 350 degrees - 35 minutes or until knife comes out clean when inserted.

LEMON MERINGUE PIE
(w/homemade pie crust)

HOMEMADE PIE CRUST
1 cup all-purpose flour
1 teaspoon sugar
1/8 teaspoon salt
1/2 cup shortening
3 Tablespoons ice water

Combine flour, sugar, and salt. Cut shortening into flour with pastry blender. Add ice water, 1 teaspoon at a time, until desired consistency for dough is reached. All of the ice water may not be used. Mix well. (Do not overmix.) Roll out dough on lightly floured wax paper. Form into pie pan. Freeze crust 12 minutes.

Bake at 400 degrees - 7-8 minutes or until golden brown.

FILLING
1-1/2 cups sugar
2-1/4 cups milk
1/2 teaspoon salt
6 Tablespoons cornstarch
4 egg yolks (beaten)
1/2 cup fresh lemon juice
4 Tablespoons butter

Combine sugar, 1 cup milk, and salt in a large saucepan. Heat until first boiling bubble breaks the surface. In a small mixing bowl, combine remaining milk and cornstarch. Whisk to blend. Gradually pour into boiling mixture. Cook over medium heat until filling is thick. Remove from heat. Stir in egg yolks, one at a time, beating after each addition. Add lemon juice. Cook over medium heat until mixture begins to bubble. Stir in butter. Let set at room temperature until filling is lukewarm.

MERINGUE
4 egg whites
1/2 teaspoon salt
1/2 cup sugar

Beat egg whites until frothy. Add salt. Add sugar, 1 Tablespoon at a time, beating after each addition. Beat until mixture is a glossy white. Spread to edge of pie.

Bake at 325 degrees - 12-15 minutes.

COCONUT PIE

1 (9-inch) pastry crust
  (baked)
1 cup sugar
5 Tablespoons
  cornstarch
1-1/4 cups milk
3/4 cup evaporated
  milk
3 egg yolks
1/4 cup margarine
1 teaspoon vanilla
1-1/4 cups shredded
  coconut
1 cup whipping cream
3 Tablespoons
  powdered sugar

Combine sugar, cornstarch, and milk in a medium saucepan. Whisk to blend. Add yolks, 1 at a time, beating after each addition. Cook over medium heat until mixture becomes thick and creamy. Remove from heat. Stir in margarine, vanilla, and coconut. Beat to blend. Pour filling into crust. Cool at room temperature 30 minutes. Refrigerate 1 hour.

Beat whipping cream until foamy. Gradually add powdered sugar, beating on high speed to form soft peaks. Spread whipped cream over chilled pie. Chill until ready to serve.

Do you remember hiding behind the barn to smoke an old homemade corn pipe that Grandpa helped you make?

SWEET POTATO PIE

2 (9-inch) pastry shells
2 cups sweet potatoes
  (cooked)
2 cups sugar
1/2 cup butter
3 eggs
1 teaspoon cinnamon
1/2 teaspoon nutmeg
1/2 teaspoon allspice
2 teaspoons vanilla
  extract
3/4 cup evaporated
  milk
1 Tablespoon all-
  purpose flour

Pastry shells should be kept in freezer at least 15 minutes prior to baking.

Bake at 400 degrees 7-8 minutes.

Whip potatoes until creamy. In a separate bowl, cream sugar and butter. Add eggs, 1 at a time, beating after each addition. Stir in spices, vanilla, milk, and flour. Mix thoroughly. Spoon filling into partially baked pie crust.

Bake at 325 degrees - 40-50 minutes or until filling is firm to touch.

PECAN PIE

1 (9-inch) pastry shell
1 cup sugar
1 Tablespoon flour
1 cup light corn syrup
1/2 cup butter
4 eggs (beaten)
1 teaspoon vanilla
  extract
1/4 teaspoon salt
1-1/3 cups pecans
  (lightly toasted)

Keep pie crust frozen until ready to bake.

Bake pastry shell at 400 degrees 7-8 minutes.

Combine sugar, flour, corn syrup, and butter in a small saucepan. Cook over medium heat, stirring constantly, until sugar dissolves. Allow mixture to cool 10 minutes. Add eggs, vanilla, salt, and pecans to filling. Mix thoroughly. Pour filling into pastry shell.

Bake at 325 degrees - 50-55 minutes.

Should crust brown too quickly, make a tent-shape from foil to cover for remainder of baking. Foil should not touch top of pie.

CHEESECAKE PECAN PIE

h) deep dish pie

ɔoon all-purpose
ɪr

Freeze pie crust 15-20 minutes before baking. Sprinkle flour over bottom of pie crust.

Bake at 400 degrees 7-8 minutes.

I
1 (8-ounce) package cream cheese (softened)
1 large egg
1/3 cup granulated sugar
2 teaspoons vanilla extract
1/4 teaspoon salt

Combine all ingredients in **Layer I**. Beat to blend well. Spoon into bottom of pie crust.

LAYER II
1 cup coarsely chopped pecans
3 large eggs
1 cup light corn syrup
2 Tablespoons light brown sugar
1 Tablespoon all-purpose flour

Combine all ingredients in **Layer II**. Spoon over **Layer I**.

Bake at 350 degrees - 35-40 minutes or until knife comes out clean when inserted.

APPLE COBBLER

CREAM CHEESE PASTRY

2 cups all-purpose flour

2 Tablespoons sugar

1 teaspoon salt

1/2 teaspoon nutmeg

7 Tablespoons shortening

1 Tablespoon butter

2 (8-ounce) packages cream cheese (softened)

5-6 Tablespoons cold water

Sift flour, sugar, salt, and nutmeg together. Cut shortening, butter, and cream cheese into flour with a pastry blender. Mixture should be crumbly. Add water by sprinkling 1 Tablespoon at a time over dough. Use a fork to blend water in (do not over mix). Form dough into a ball and cover with plastic wrap. Chill while filling is prepared.

Divide dough into two equal sections. Roll out 1/2 of dough and form into bottom of a buttered 9-inch square glass dish.

Bake at 400 degrees 10 minutes.

FILLING

3 large apples (peeled & finely chopped)

2 teaspoons cinnamon

1/2 teaspoon allspice

1 cup sugar

3 Tablespoons all-purpose flour

1 cup whipping cream

1 teaspoon vanilla extract

Combine all ingredients and mix thoroughly. Spoon mixture over bottom half of dough. Roll out remaining dough. Cut into 1-inch strips. Arrange in crisscross pattern over top of filling.

Bake at 400 degrees 10 minutes. Reduce heat to 275 degrees and bake 40-45 minutes.

BLUEBERRY PIE

1 (9-inch) pie crust
2-1/2 cups blueberries
3/4 cup sugar
1 cup sour cream
3 Tablespoons all-
purpose flour
1 teaspoon vanilla
extract
1/4 teaspoon salt
1 egg (beaten)

Freeze crust 15 minutes.

Bake at 400 degrees 7-8 minutes.

Sprinkle blueberries with sugar. Set aside.

Combine sour cream, flour, vanilla, salt, and egg. Beat to blend. Gently fold in blueberries. Pour mixture into pie crust.

Bake at 400 degrees - 25-30 minutes.

TOPPING
3 Tablespoons all-
purpose flour
2 Tablespoons sugar
1/2 teaspoon cinnamon
3 Tablespoons
margarine (melted)
1/2 cup finely chopped
pecans (lightly
toasted)

Combine topping ingredients to make a crumbly mixture. Sprinkle over baked pie. Return to oven.

Bake at 400 degrees - 10 minutes.

EASY PEACH PIE

2 (9-inch) pastry shells
1 teaspoon all-purpose
   flour
1/2 teaspoon nutmeg
4 cups sliced peaches
1 cup 7-Up
1/2 cup granulated sugar
1/4 cup light brown sugar
2 Tablespoons butter
3 Tablespoons cornstarch
2 teaspoons cinnamon
1/2 teaspoon allspice

Freeze crust 15 minutes before baking.

Bake at 400 degrees 7-8 minutes.

Combine flour and nutmeg. Sprinkle over bottom portion of partially baked pastry shell.

Combine peaches, 7-UP, sugars, butter, and cornstarch. Cook over medium heat until mixture begins to thicken. Stir in spices. Spoon mixture into pastry shell. Top with remaining pastry. Pinch edges together. Make 4 slits in the top of crust.

Bake at 350 degrees 30-40 minutes.

Apples or pears may be substituted for peaches.

Do you remember the sweet smell of honeysuckles in early spring?

FRUIT PIE

2 (9-inch) pie shells (baked)

1 (16-ounce) can strawberry pie filling

3/4 cup sugar

1 (8.25-ounce) can crushed pineapple w/juice

2 Tablespoons cornstarch

1 teaspoon red food coloring

1 (3-ounce) package strawberry gelatin

4 bananas (sliced)

2 teaspoons lemon juice

1 cup coarsely chopped pecans

1 (8-ounce) carton frozen whipped topping

Combine pie filling, sugar, pineapple, cornstarch, and food coloring in a large saucepan. Cook over medium heat until mixture thickens. Remove from heat. Stir mixture 3-4 minutes. Add gelatin. Mix thoroughly. Let mixture cool to lukewarm temperature. Stir in remaining ingredients. Spoon mixture into pie crusts. Top with dollop of prepared topping before serving.

BREAD PUDDING
(w/vanilla-rum sauce)

6 cups French bread
1 cup evaporated milk
1 cup whipping cream
3 eggs
1 cup sugar
1/2 cup butter (divided)
1 Tablespoon vanilla
   extract

Cube bread into 1-inch pieces. (Bread should be 2-3 days old.) Combine milk and cream. Pour over bread cubes. Let set 25 minutes.

Combine eggs, sugar, 1/4 cup butter, and vanilla extract. Beat until creamy. Pour mixture over soaked bread. Spoon bread into a greased 8x8-inch pan. Set pan in larger container with 1-inch of water in bottom. Slice remaining butter into 1/8 inch pieces. Dot top of pudding with butter.

Bake at 325 degrees - 1 hour or until knife comes out clean when inserted.

Let set 25 minutes before serving.

VANILLA-RUM SAUCE

1/3 cup granulated
   sugar
1/3 cup brown sugar
3/4 cup evaporated milk
1 Tablespoon warm
   water
2 teaspoons cornstarch
1/4 cup butter
2 teaspoons vanilla
   extract
1/2 teaspoon rum
   extract

Combine sugars, milk, water, and cornstarch in a medium saucepan. Cook over medium heat until mixture begins to thicken. Add butter. Reduce to low heat. Whisk until butter melts. Remove from heat. Stir in vanilla and rum extract.

CARAMEL-TOFFEE ICE CREAM DESSERT
(w/caramel sauce)

1-1/2 cups graham cracker crumbs

5 Tablespoons butter (melted)

1 quart vanilla ice cream (softened)

1 (6-ounce) package toffee pieces

Line a 2-quart bowl with a large square of plastic wrap that has been coated with non stick vegetable spray. Combine crumbs and butter. Press mixture into a bowl. Combine ice cream and toffee pieces. Mix lightly. Spoon over crumbs. Cover with plastic wrap and freeze. Remove from freezer 6-7 minutes before serving. Lift mixture from bowl. Cut into wedges.

CARAMEL SAUCE

2 cups sugar

1/4 cup light corn syrup

1/4 cup water

2 cups chilled heavy cream

3/4 cup chopped pecans (lightly toasted)

Combine sugar, corn syrup, and water in a medium saucepan. Bring to a boil over high heat. Boil until medium golden in color (approximately 10 minutes). Remove from heat and gradually fold in cream, stirring constantly. The mixture will be very bubbly. Return to heat and bring to a boil for 8-10 minutes. Cool. Pour over dessert.

Sprinkle with toasted pecans.

More cream may be added. Sauce should be thick but remain of a pouring consistency.

CHEESECAKE WESLEY

CRUST

1 cup graham cracker
   crumbs
1/2 stick butter (melted)
1/4 cup sugar

Combine all ingredients. Press firmly into a spring form pan coated with cooking spray.

CHEESECAKE

2 (8-ounce) packages
   cream cheese
   (softened)
3 eggs
1 (14.5-ounce) can
   condensed milk
1/4 teaspoon salt
1/4 cup lemon juice

Beat cream cheese until light and fluffy. Add eggs, beating after each addition. Add condensed milk and salt. Beat to mix. Stir in lemon juice. Pour into prepared pan.

Bake at 300 degrees - 30 minutes.

TOPPING

2 cups sour cream
1/4 cup sugar
1/4 teaspoon vanilla

Combine topping ingredients. Pour over cheesecake. Bake 5 additional minutes. Cool 30 minutes. Refrigerate overnight. Remove from pan.

Favorite topping may be added after cheesecake has been removed from pan.

CHOCOLATE ECLAIR DESSERT

1/2 cup butter
1 cup 7-UP
1 cup all-purpose flour
1/2 teaspoon
cinnamon
1/4 teaspoon salt
4 eggs (beaten)
2 (3.4-ounce)
packages vanilla
pudding mix
3/4 cup milk
3/4 cup evaporated
milk
1 (8-ounce) package
cream cheese
(softened)
1 (12-ounce) carton
frozen whipped
topping (thawed)

In a medium saucepan, melt butter. Add 7-Up. Bring to a rolling boil. Stir in flour, cinnamon, and salt. Beat until mixture holds together. Cool 6-7 minutes. Add eggs, 1 at a time, beating after addition. Spread mixture into an ungreased 15x10x1-inch jelly roll pan. Pierce dough lightly at 3-inch intervals.

Bake at 350 degrees - 30-40 minutes.

Combine pudding mix, milk, and cream cheese. Beat until thoroughly blended. Spread mixture over cooled pastry. Spread topping over pudding.

CHOCOLATE GLAZE

3/4 cup semi-sweet
chocolate chips
2 Tablespoons
shortening
1 cup powdered sugar
3-4 Tablespoons milk

Melt chocolate chips and shortening in a medium saucepan. Add sugar and milk to make a glaze. Drizzle glaze over topping. Refrigerate 2 hours.

PEACH CRISP SURPRISE

2 cups peaches (peeled & sliced)

1 Tablespoon lemon juice

2/3 cup chopped pitted dates

1/2 cup butter

2/3 cup granulated sugar

1-2/3 cups all-purpose flour

1/4 teaspoon salt

1 teaspoon cinnamon

1/4 teaspoon nutmeg

2/3 cup quick cooking rolled oats

4 Tablespoons peanut butter

Sprinkle peaches with lemon juice. Combine peaches and dates. Layer over bottom of a greased 13x9x2-inch cake pan. Set aside.

Cream butter and sugar until soft and fluffy. Combine flour, salt, and spices to make a crumbly mixture. Stir in oats and peanut butter. (Do not over mix.) Spoon over fruit mixture.

Bake at 350 degrees - 20-25 minutes.

Do you remember playing hide and seek around the corners of the house?

NANA'S STRAWBERRY SHORTCAKE

2 pints strawberries
(sliced)
1 cup sugar
2 cups all-purpose
flour
2-1/2 teaspoons
baking powder
1/4 teaspoon salt
1/4 teaspoon
cinnamon
6 Tablespoons butter
(softened)
2/3 cup half & half
1 (8-ounce) carton
prepared whipped
topping

Sprinkle strawberries with 1/2 cup sugar. Set aside.

Sift remaining sugar, flour, baking powder, salt, and cinnamon. Cut in butter until mixture is crumbly. Stir in half & half to make a smooth dough. Turn onto a generously floured board. Knead 1-2 minutes or until dough is smooth. Roll out into an 8-inch circle. Place on a greased baking sheet.

Bake at 375 degrees - 25 minutes, or until golden brown.

Split shortcake while still warm. Drain strawberries. Fill with 1/2 berries. Pile remaining berries over top of shortcake.

Top with dollops of whipped topping just before serving.

desserts

STRAWBERRY SAUCE - Crush 2 cups fresh strawberries. In a small saucepan, combine berries, 3/4 cup sugar, 2 Tablespoons cornstarch, 2 Tablespoons butter, 1-1/2 teaspoons lemon juice, and 1 cup Sprite or 7-UP. Cook over medium heat until mixture thickens. Use wire whisk for a smooth consistency.

LEMON-BLUEBERRY SAUCE - Combine 1 cup water, 1/2 cup sugar, and 1 Tablespoon cornstarch. Stir until sugar and cornstarch have dissolved. Heat on medium-low until mixture thickens. Stir in 2 Tablespoons margarine, 2 teaspoons lemon juice, and 1/2 teaspoon lemon rind. Whisk to blend. Fold in 1 cup fresh blueberries.

CUSTARD SAUCE - In a blender, combine 4 egg yolks, 1/4 cup sugar, 1/8 teaspoon salt, and 1-1/4 cups milk. Blend on high speed 1 minute. Pour mixture into a saucepan and cook over low heat until mixture thickens enough to coat metal spoon. Stir in 1/4 teaspoon almond extract.

EASY CHOCOLATE SAUCE - Combine 4 (1-ounce) chocolate squares and 3/4 cup milk in a double boiler. Heat until chocolate melts. Stir in 1 cup sugar, 1/8 teaspoon cinnamon, 1/8 teaspoon salt, and 5 Tablespoons butter. Mix thoroughly. Seal and refrigerate. Sauce will keep for several weeks.

CHOCOLATE WHIPPED CREAM - Heat 1 cup whipping cream until first boiling bubble breaks the surface. Remove from heat. Break 2 (1.55 ounce) plain chocolate candy bars into small pieces. Add to whipping cream. Whisk until smooth. Pour into mixing bowl. Stir occasionally while mixture cools - 1 hour. Beat with electric mixer until whipped cream is stiff.

cakes

almost scratch cake w/chocolate frosting, **220**

chocolate brownie cake, **221**

coconut cake w/sour cream frosting, **222**

italian cake w/cream cheese frosting, **223**

praline pan cake w/praline icing, **224**

fresh strawberry cake w/glaze, **225**

plain pound cake, **226**

chocolate pound cake w/chocolate glaze, **227**

coconut pecan pound cake, **228**

marbled pound cake, **229**

sweet potato spice pound cake, **230**

vanilla wafer cake, **231**

lemon pecan fruit cake, **232**

mama bea's jelly roll, **233**

funnel cakes, **234**

ALMOST SCRATCH CAKE
(w/chocolate frosting)

1 (18-1/4-ounce) box
    yellow cake mix
1/2 cup sugar
4 eggs
3/4 cup cooking oil
1 teaspoon vanilla
    extract
1 cup orange juice

In a large mixing bowl, combine cake mix, sugar, eggs, cooking oil, and vanilla extract. Mix thoroughly. Pour orange juice into mixture. Beat to blend. Spoon batter into a greased 13x9x2-inch cake pan.

Bake at 325 degrees - 30-35 minutes.

CHOCOLATE
FROSTING
1-1/2 sticks butter
    (melted)
3 Tablespoons cocoa
1 (16-ounce) box
    powdered sugar
2-3 Tablespoons milk
1 teaspoon vanilla

Melt butter. Sift cocoa and powdered sugar. Stir into melted butter. Add milk, a Tablespoon at a time, mixing after each addition. Add vanilla. Beat until smooth.

Additional milk may be used to reach desired consistency.

"June Bug" reminisces about growing up in the Delta of the Mississippi River. He was the second of five children. "Christmas was always a special time. 'Mamadear' made sure that everyone had their favorite sweet treat for Christmas dinner. Each of us had a sweet tooth for a particular dessert. 'Anyann' loved chocolate cake with chocolate frosting, 'Sha wul' always wanted a layered coconut cake, 'Beauty' favored chocolate cake with white icing, 'Bokie' must have meringue pie, and I wanted a jelly cake and a sweet potato pie."

CHOCOLATE BROWNIE CAKE

BATTER
1/2 cup butter (softened)
2 cups sugar
2 eggs
1 teaspoon vanilla extract
2 cups all-purpose flour
1 teaspoon baking powder
1/2 teaspoon baking soda
1/4 teaspoon salt
1 cup milk

Cream butter and sugar until blended. In a separate bowl, whisk eggs until creamy. Add to creamed mixture and mix thoroughly. Sift dry ingredients into a separate bowl. Alternately add milk and dry ingredients to creamed mixture, beating after each addition.

Pour 1/2 batter into a greased 13x9x2-inch pan. Drizzle 1/2 fudge swirl filling evenly over batter. Pour remaining batter into pan and spoon remaining fudge swirl mixture over top of cake.

Bake at 350 degrees - 50-60 minutes.

FUDGE SWIRL FILLING
1 (8-ounce) package cream cheese (softened)
1 egg
1/4 cup sugar
3 Tablespoons milk
2 Tablespoons butter (melted)
1 teaspoon vanilla extract
1 Tablespoon cornstarch
4 (1-ounce) unsweetened chocolate squares (melted)

Combine cream cheese, egg, and sugar in a large mixing bowl. Beat until mixture is light and creamy. Add milk, butter, and vanilla extract. Mix well. Stir in cornstarch until thoroughly mixed. Add chocolate. (Chocolate should be cooled slightly before adding to mixture.) Beat with mixer to blend.

FROSTING
2 (1-ounce) squares unsweetened chocolate
1/4 cup butter
3-1/2 cups powdered sugar
1/3 cup milk
1 teaspoon vanilla extract

Melt chocolate. Stir in butter immediately. Allow chocolate mixture to cool slightly. Add powdered sugar and milk. Beat to blend. Stir in vanilla extract. Cake should be thoroughly cooled before frosting.

COCONUT CAKE
(w/sour cream frosting)

1 cup butter
1/2 cup shortening
1 cup granulated sugar
1/2 cup powdered sugar
1 (3-ounce) package cream cheese (softened)
4 eggs
1 cup warm milk
2-1/4 cups all-purpose flour
1 Tablespoon baking powder
1/4 teaspoon salt
2 teaspoons vanilla extract

Cream butter, shortening, sugars, and cream cheese. Add eggs and milk. Beat to blend.

Sift dry ingredients. Add to creamed mixture. Stir in vanilla. Beat to blend.

SOUR CREAM FROSTING

1/2 stick butter (softened)
1 (16-ounce) box powdered sugar
1/2 teaspoon cream of tartar
3/4 cup sour cream
1 teaspoon vanilla extract
2 cups shredded fresh coconut (lightly toasted)

Whip butter until creamy. Sift sugar and cream of tartar together. Combine with butter mixture. Stir in sour cream, vanilla extract, and 1 cup coconut. Spread over cooled cake. Sprinkle remaining coconut over top and sides of frosted cake.

ITALIAN CREAM CAKE
(w/cream cheese frosting)

3/4 teaspoon cream of
tartar
4 eggs (separated)
1 cup buttermilk
1 teaspoon baking soda
1/2 cup butter (softened)
1/2 cup shortening
2-1/4 cups sugar
2 teaspoons vanilla extract
2 cups all-purpose flour
1/4 teaspoon baking
powder
1/4 teaspoon salt
3/4 cup flaked coconut
(lightly toasted)

Beat egg whites and cream of tartar to form soft peaks. Set aside.

Combine buttermilk and baking soda. Set aside.

Blend butter, shortening, sugar, and vanilla until creamy. Add egg yolks, 1 at a time, beating after each addition.

Sift dry ingredients. Alternately add buttermilk and dry ingredients to butter mixture, beating after each addition.

Begin and end with dry ingredients. Stir in coconut. Fold in beaten egg whites. Pour batter into (3) 9-inch greased cake pans.

Bake at 325 degrees - 25-30 minutes.

CREAM CHEESE FROSTING
1 (16-ounce) box
powdered sugar
1/2 cup butter (softened)
1 (8-ounce) package
cream cheese
(softened)
1 teaspoon vanilla extract
1-1/4 cups pecans (lightly
toasted)

Sift sugar. Blend butter and cream cheese. Add powdered sugar. Blend thoroughly. Stir in vanilla and pecans. Mix well.

Spread between layers and over top and sides of cooled cake.

PRALINE PAN CAKE
(w/praline icing)

2-1/4 cups all-purpose
  flour
2 teaspoons baking
  powder
1/2 teaspoon salt
2 cups sugar
2/3 cup shortening
1/4 cup butter
1-1/3 cups milk
3 eggs (beaten)
1 teaspoon vanilla
  extract

Sift dry ingredients. Add shortening and butter. Beat on low speed until mixture is crumbly.

Pour milk over shortening mixture. Mix on low speed 4 minutes. Add eggs and vanilla. Beat 2 minutes. Pour into a lightly greased 13x9x2-inch pan.

Bake at 300 degrees - 40-45 minutes.

PRALINE ICING

1 stick butter (melted)
1 cup light brown sugar
  (firmly packed)
1 cup chopped pecans
  (lightly toasted)
1/2 cup milk

Combine butter, brown sugar, and pecans. Add milk, 1 Tablespoon at a time, until desired consistency is reached for spreading. Beat to blend. Spread over hot cake. Broil on middle rack to lightly brown icing.

Do you remember playing outside and filling mason jars with "lightning bugs" at twilight while Mama, Papa, and the neighbors talked about adult things?

FRESH STRAWBERRY CAKE
(w/glaze)

1 (18-1/4-ounce)
  package white
  cake mix
1-1/4 cups crushed
  strawberries
2 Tablespoons all-
  purpose flour
1 (3-ounce) package
  strawberry-flavored
  gelatin
1/2 cup vegetable oil
4 eggs
1 teaspoon vanilla
1/2 cup 7-UP

Combine all ingredients. Beat to blend. Spoon batter into a greased bundt pan.

Bake at 325 degrees 50 minutes.

GLAZE
1 stick butter
3-1/2 cups powdered
  sugar
1/2 cup crushed
  strawberries
1/4 cup 7-UP

Whip butter until creamy. Stir in powdered sugar and strawberries. Mix thoroughly. Add 7-UP. Mix well. Drizzle over warm cake.

Do you remember Grandpa giving you enough money to buy a moon pie and a cold drink?

PLAIN POUND CAKE

2 sticks butter
(softened)

1/2 cup vegetable
shortening

1 (3-ounce) package
cream cheese
(softened)

3 cups sugar

6 eggs

3 cups all-purpose
flour

1 teaspoon baking
powder

1 cup milk

1 teaspoon lemon
extract

1 teaspoon vanilla
extract

1/2 teaspoon rum
extract

Beat butter, shortening, cream cheese, and sugar until creamy. Add eggs, 1 at a time. Sift flour and baking powder. Alternately add milk and flour to creamed mixture. Add lemon, vanilla, and rum extracts. Beat to blend. Spoon mixture into a greased bundt pan.

Bake at 325 degrees - 1 hour 30 minutes.

Do you remember hav-ing a tree house that was off limits to those pesky girls?

CHOCOLATE POUND CAKE
(w/chocolate glaze)

1 cup buttermilk

1 teaspoon baking soda

2 sticks butter (softened)

2 cups granulated sugar

3/4 cup brown sugar (firmly packed)

5 eggs

2-1/4 cups all-purpose flour

1/2 teaspoon baking powder

7 Tablespoons cocoa

2 teaspoons vanilla extract

Add baking soda to buttermilk. Set aside.

Combine sugars and butter. Beat to blend until creamy. Add eggs, 1 at a time, to creamed mixture. Beat 30 seconds after each addition.

Sift remaining dry ingredients together. Alternately add buttermilk and flour to mixture. Beat after each addition. Begin and end with dry ingredients. Stir in vanilla. Spoon batter into a greased and floured 10-inch tube pan.

Bake at 325 degrees - 1 hour 30 minutes.

ICING

2 (1-ounce) squares unsweetened chocolate

1/3 cup butter

2 cups powdered sugar

2 teaspoons vanilla extract

3-4 Tablespoons hot water

Combine chocolate and butter in a small saucepan. Heat over low temperature until chocolate is melted. Remove from heat. Stir in sugar and vanilla. Beat to blend. Stir in water, 1 Tablespoon at a time. Use only enough water to make icing smooth and creamy. Drizzle over warm cake.

COCONUT PECAN POUND CAKE

1·(18.25-ounce) box
  yellow cake mix
1 (3.4-ounce) package
  instant vanilla
  pudding
1-1/4 cups sugar
4 eggs (beaten)
8 ounces sour cream
2/3 cup orange juice
1/2 cup vegetable oil
1 teaspoon vanilla
  extract
1/2 teaspoon lemon
  extract
1/4 teaspoon almond
  extract
1 cup chopped pecans
  (lightly toasted)
1/2 cup grated coconut
  (lightly toasted)

Combine dry ingredients. Add liquid ingredients. Beat to blend thoroughly. Fold in pecans and coconut. Pour batter into a greased bundt pan.

Bake at 325 degrees - 1 hour 30 minutes.

GLAZE

1 cup powdered sugar
1 Tablespoon butter
  (melted)
1/2 teaspoon vanilla
  extract
2 Tablespoons milk

Let cake cool 10 minutes before removing from pan. Pour glaze over warm cake.

MARBLED POUND CAKE

3 Tablespoons graham
    cracker crumbs
1 cup buttermilk
1/2 teaspoon baking soda
1-1/2 cups butter
    (softened)
2 cups granulated sugar
1 cup brown sugar
5 eggs
3 cups all-purpose flour
1/2 teaspoon baking
    powder
1/4 teaspoon salt
2 teaspoons vanilla extract
1 (1-ounce) square
    semi-sweet chocolate
1 Tablespoon shortening

Coat inside of bundt pan with Baker's Joy spray (combination of flour and oil in a spray). Lightly sprinkle bottom and sides of bundt pan with graham cracker crumbs. Set pan in oven preheated to 350 degrees. Leave 10 minutes. Remove from oven and set aside.

In a small container, add soda to buttermilk. Set aside.

In a large mixing bowl, beat butter and sugars until creamy. (approximately 7 minutes). Add eggs, 1 at a time, beating after each addition. Sift dry ingredients together. Alternately add dry ingredients and buttermilk to butter mixture, beginning and ending with dry mixture. Stir in vanilla.

In a small saucepan, heat shortening and chocolate until chocolate melts. Add 1 cup batter to chocolate. Blend thoroughly. Pour 1/3 plain batter over bottom of prepared cake pan. (Smooth batter after each layer.) Spoon 1/2 chocolate batter into pan. Make another layer of plain batter. Add remaining chocolate mix. Top with remaining batter. Insert knife into batter and gently swirl to create marbled pattern.

Bake at 350 degrees - 30 minutes. Reduce heat to 325 degrees 1 hour or until toothpick comes out clean when inserted into middle of cake.

SWEET POTATO SPICE POUND CAKE

2 cups cooked sweet potatoes

1 cup vegetable oil

1/3 cup orange juice

2 teaspoons vanilla extract

1 teaspoon butter flavoring

5 eggs

3 cups all purpose flour

2 cups granulated sugar

1 cup brown sugar (firmly packed)

2 teaspoons baking powder

1/2 teaspoon baking soda

1/2 teaspoon salt

2 teaspoons cinnamon

1 teaspoon nutmeg

1 teaspoon allspice

Whip sweet potatoes until consistency is very smooth. Combine oil, orange juice, and flavorings to sweet potatoes. Add eggs, 1 at a time, beating after each addition.

Sift dry ingredients together. Add to sweet potato mixture. Beat to blend. Spoon batter into a 10-inch tube pan.

Bake at 325 degrees - 1 hour 30 minutes.

Do you remember chasing after the ice truck for a few chips of ice on a hot summer day?

VANILLA WAFER CAKE

1 (13-ounce) box
vanilla wafers

2 cups chopped
pecans (lightly
toasted)

1 (7-ounce) package
flake coconut

1-1/2 cups granulated
sugar

3/4 cup butter

6 eggs

1/2 cup milk

1 teaspoon vanilla
extract

Crush wafers into fine crumbs. (Use blender to pulverize wafers.) Mix with pecans and coconut.

In a separate bowl, cream sugar and butter together. Add eggs, beating after each addition. Stir in milk and vanilla. Combine with wafer mixture. Blend well. Spoon mixture into a greased and floured tube pan.

Bake at 325 degrees - 1 hour.

Do you remember being told that if you were not "good," the greasy man or "boogie man" would get you?

LEMON PECAN FRUIT CAKE

6 eggs (separated)

1 pound light brown sugar

1 pound butter

4 cups all-purpose flour

1 teaspoon baking powder

2 ounces lemon extract

4 cups chopped pecans (lightly toasted)

1/2 pound candied pineapple

1/2 pound candied cherries

Beat yolks until creamy. In a separate bowl, cream sugar and butter. Add egg yolks. Beat to blend thoroughly. Add 3 cups flour, baking powder, and lemon extract.

Dredge pecans, pineapple, and cherries in remaining cup of flour. Fold nuts and fruits into creamed mixture. Beat egg whites until foamy. Add egg whites and mix thoroughly. Cover and set in refrigerator overnight. Beat to mix thoroughly before pouring into (2) 9x5x2-inch loaf pans lined with wax paper.

Bake at 250 degrees - 2 hours.

Baked loaves may be soaked with wine or bourbon. Wrap in cloth. Freeze in ziplock bags.

MAMA BEA'S JELLYROLL

5 eggs (separated)
1-1/4 cups powdered
  sugar
1 Tablespoon milk
1 Tablespoon ice water
1 teaspoon vanilla
  extract
1 cup all-purpose flour
1 teaspoon baking
  powder
3/4 teaspoon salt
1/4 teaspoon cinnamon
2 cups jelly

Beat egg whites until stiff. In a separate bowl, combine egg yolks and sugar. Beat to blend. Add milk, ice water, and vanilla. Beat until creamy.

Sift dry ingredients together. Sprinkle over egg whites. Blend mixture together. Combine with egg yolk mixture. Fold to blend. Spoon batter into a 15x10x1-inch jellyroll pan that has been lined with wax paper. Smooth dough over paper.

Bake at 350 degrees - 20 minutes.

Let cake cool 15 minutes. Turn onto smooth damp cloth. Remove paper and spread with jelly. Carefully roll up from 10-inch end.

1/2 cup powdered sugar may be sifted over roll.

Do you remember being sent to a neighbor's house to borrow a cup of sugar, but always taking them something in return, like a pint of mayhaw jelly?

FUNNEL CAKES

1-1/2 cups milk
2 eggs (beaten)
4 Tablespoons
   granulated sugar
3 Tablespoons light
   brown sugar
2 cups all-purpose
   flour
2 teaspoons baking
   powder
3/4 teaspoon cinnamon
1/2 teaspoon salt
3 cups vegetable oil
1 cup powdered sugar

Combine milk, eggs, and sugars. Beat vigorously to blend thoroughly. Sift remaining dry ingredients together. Gradually add dry ingredients to liquid mixture. Beat until smooth and creamy.

Heat vegetable oil to 350 degrees in a 12-inch skillet. Close end of funnel with finger. Pour 1/2 cup mixture into funnel. Place funnel over center of skillet and open the end. Move in a tight circular movement around skillet. Fry batter until golden brown (2-3 minutes). Using a wide spatula, turn batter once to brown on both sides.

As soon as cakes are removed, lay on paper towels and sprinkle generously with powdered sugar.

cookies and candy

chocolate-vanilla chip cookies, 236

orange slice jumbles, 237

applesauce walnut cookies, 238

malted festival cookies, 239

peanut butter cookies / oatmeal raisin cookies, 240

granola raisin cookies / german lady cookies, 241

date pin wheel cookies, 242

granny's syrup cakes, 243

gingersnaps / coconut macaroons, 244

sugar cookies, 245

pecan puffs/ orange balls, 246

caramel brownies, 247

chocolate pecan pie bars, 248

honey bars, 249

frosted fingers, 250

strawberry cheesecake bars, 251

aunt sis' congo bars /quick dessert bars, 252

creamy vanilla fudge / quick fudge, 253

creamy pecan pralines / pecan pralines, 254

martha washington balls, 255

CHOCOLATE-VANILLA COOKIES

1 stick margarine
1 stick butter
3/4 cup brown sugar
   (firmly packed)
3/4 cup granulated
   sugar
3/4 cup quick cooking
   rolled oats
2 eggs
1 teaspoon vanilla
   extract
2 cups all-purpose
   flour
1 teaspoon baking
   soda
1/4 teaspoon salt
1 cup semi-sweet
   chocolate chips
1 cup coarsely grated
   white chocolate

Whip margarine, butter, sugars, oats, eggs, and vanilla on medium speed until creamy.

Sift all dry ingredients. Add to creamed mixture. Mix only enough to blend thoroughly.

Stir in chocolate chips and white chocolate. Mix well. Drop from heaping teaspoon onto ungreased cookie sheet.

Bake at 325 degrees - 12-13 minutes or until lightly browned around edges.

Vanilla chips may be substituted for white chocolate. One cup coarsely chopped pecans may be added for variety.

Do you remember easing up to catch a "mosquito hawk" perched on the fence? Junior, who grew up in the 1950's, recalls luring these "mosquito hawks" to perch on an out-stretched stick by singing,

Mister Mosquito Hawk, beautiful and free,
Please don't fly away unless you also take me.
I'm your friend; this you can see.
Mister Mosquito Hawk, you're so exciting to me.

ORANGE SLICE JUMBLES

3/4 cup brown sugar
3/4 cup granulated
   sugar
1/2 cup butter
3 eggs
1 Tablespoon water
1 teaspoon vanilla
   flavoring
1 Tablespoon grated
   orange peel
3 cups all-purpose flour
1 teaspoon baking
   soda
1/4 teaspoon salt
1 cup raisins
3/4 cup chopped
   pecans
1 pound orange slice
   candy (chopped)

Cream sugars and butter together. Add eggs, water, vanilla flavoring, and orange peel.

Sift dry ingredients. Add pecans and raisins to flour mixture. Toss to coat. Add to creamed mixture and blend thoroughly. Stir in orange slices. Drop from teaspoon onto ungreased baking sheet.

Bake at 375 degrees - 10-12 minutes.

APPLESAUCE WALNUT COOKIES

1/2 cup shortening
1/2 cup margarine
1 cup brown sugar
(packed)
1/2 cup granulated
sugar
2 eggs
1 teaspoon vanilla
extract
2 cups all-purpose
flour
1 teaspoon baking
soda
1/2 teaspoon salt
2 teaspoons cinnamon
1 teaspoon ground
cloves
1-1/2 cups applesauce
1 cup chopped dates
1 cup chopped walnuts
1/2 cup quick cooking
rolled oats

Combine shortening, margarine, sugars, eggs, and vanilla. Beat until creamy.

In a separate bowl, sift all dry ingredients. Add to creamed mixture. Stir applesauce, dates, walnuts, and rolled oats into batter. Drop from teaspoon onto ungreased baking sheet.

Bake at 325 degrees - 12-15 minutes.

ICING
2 cup powdered sugar
1-2 Tablespoons milk
1 teaspoon lemon
juice

Combine powdered sugar, milk, and lemon juice. Add milk 1 teaspoon at a time until desired consistency is reached. Drizzle icing over warm cookies.

MALTED FESTIVAL COOKIES

1/2 cup shortening
1/2 cup butter
1-1/4 cups brown sugar (firmly packed)
3/4 cup quick cooking rolled oats
1/2 cup malted milk powder
2 Tablespoons chocolate syrup
2 teaspoons vanilla extract
2 eggs (slightly beaten)
2 cups all-purpose flour
1 teaspoon baking soda
1/4 teaspoon salt
2 cups semi-sweet chocolate chips
1/2 cup chopped pecans

Cream shortening, butter, and brown sugar together. Mixture should be very creamy. Add oats, malt powder, chocolate syrup, vanilla, and eggs. Beat to blend thoroughly.

Combine flour, soda, and salt. Gradually add to shortening mixture. Beat after each addition, but only enough to blend all ingredients.

Stir in chocolate chips and pecans. Drop from teaspoon onto ungreased baking sheet.

Bake at 375 degrees - 10-12 minutes.

A cup of peanut butter chips may be substituted for 1 cup of chocolate chips.

Do you remember playing marbles for keeps or playing fiddle sticks or jacks?

PEANUT BUTTER COOKIES

2 cups all-purpose
  flour
1/2 teaspoon baking
  soda
1 cup granulated sugar
1 cup brown sugar
  (firmly packed)
3 eggs
1/2 cup shortening
1/2 cup margarine
1 cup creamy peanut
  butter
1 Tablespoon water
1 teaspoon vanilla

Sift dry ingredients.

In a separate bowl, combine remaining ingredients. Beat to blend. Stir in dry ingredients. Form into 1-inch balls. Press down with fork to 1/2-inch the height of ball.

Bake at 325 degrees - 10-12 minutes.

OATMEAL RAISIN COOKIES

2 sticks margarine
2 cups sugar
2 teaspoons vanilla
2 eggs
1 cup finely chopped
  raisins
3/4 cup finely chopped
  pecans
2-1/2 cups all-purpose
  flour
1 teaspoon salt
1 teaspoon baking soda
2 cups oatmeal

Cream margarine, sugar, and vanilla together. Add eggs and beat until blended. Add raisins and pecans.

In a separate container, combine remaining dry ingredients. Mix well. Add to creamed mixture. Drop from teaspoon onto ungreased baking sheets.

Bake at 350 - 10-12 minutes.

GRANOLA RAISIN COOKIES

3/4 cup raisins
2 eggs
1-1/2 teaspoons vanilla
extract
1/2 cup shortening
1/2 cup butter
3/4 cup granulated sugar
3/4 cup brown sugar
(firmly packed)
2 cups all-purpose flour
1 teaspoon baking soda
1/2 teaspoon salt
1 teaspoon cinnamon
1/2 teaspoon allspice
1-1/3 cups granola cereal
3/4 cups chopped pecans

Cover raisins with warm water. Let soak 10 minutes. Drain and blot raisins dry with paper towels. Set aside.

Combine eggs, vanilla, shortening, butter, and sugars in a mixing bowl. Using an electric mixer, beat until creamy. Sift all dry ingredients into creamed mixture. Fold in raisins, granola, and pecans. Mix to blend. Drop from teaspoon onto an ungreased cookie sheet.

Bake at 325 degrees - 10-12 minutes.

"GERMAN LADY" COOKIES

2 sticks butter
1 cup granulated sugar
1 cup brown sugar
1 egg
1 cup cooking oil
1 teaspoon vanilla flavor
3-1/2 cups all-purpose
flour
1 teaspoon soda
1 teaspoon salt
1 cup crushed corn flakes
1 cup rolled oats
1/2 cup coconut
1/2 cup chopped pecans

Cream butter and sugars. Add egg, oil, and vanilla. Whisk to blend. Stir in remaining ingredients. Drop from teaspoon onto ungreased cookie sheet. Press down lightly with fork.

Bake at 350 degrees - 12 minutes.

DATE PIN WHEEL COOKIES

1 (16-ounce) box light
   brown sugar
1 cup shortening
2 eggs
3-1/4 cups flour
1 teaspoon soda
1/4 teaspoon salt
1 teaspoon cinnamon
1 teaspoon nutmeg

Combine sugar, shortening, and eggs. Beat with electric mixer until thoroughly blended. Sift dry ingredients. Gradually add flour mixture to sugar mixture. Blend well. Divide dough into 3 equal portions. Sprinkle wax paper with flour. (Dough may be hard to handle at first, but roll around on floured paper until it holds together.) Roll out a portion of dough between 2 pieces of wax paper. Roll into a rectangular shape 1/4-inch in thickness.

FILLING
1 (8-ounce) package
   dates (chopped)
1 cup chopped pecans
1/2 cup sugar
1/2 cup water

Combine all ingredients for filling in a saucepan. Cook over medium heat until mixture thickens. (Usually 8-10 minutes.) Spread 1/3 of mixture evenly over center of dough. (Do not spread filling to edge of dough. Leave a 2-inch border.) Lift edge of bottom layer of wax paper to start pinwheel. Roll like jelly-roll. Wrap wax paper and aluminum foil around each roll and freeze. When ready to bake, slice frozen dough 1/4-inch thick. Bake on ungreased cookie sheet.

Bake at 350 degrees - 8 minutes.

Unbaked date nut rolls may be frozen indefinitely and sliced as needed for baking.

GRANNY'S SYRUP CAKES

1 cup sugar
1 cup shortening
1 cup cane syrup
1 Tablespoon vanilla
    extract
2 eggs
5 cups all-purpose
    flour
1 teaspoon salt
2 teaspoons cinnamon
1 teaspoon cloves
1 teaspoon allspice
3 teaspoons soda
1 cup boiling water

Cream sugar and shortening. Add syrup and vanilla. Beat vigorously to blend ingredients. Add eggs and beat to blend. Sift dry ingredients. Combine with syrup mixture. Mix thoroughly.

Dissolve soda in boiling water. Pour over mixture. Blend thoroughly. Drop dough from teaspoon onto ungreased baking sheet. Flatten slightly with a fork.

Bake at 350 degrees - 10 minutes.

For an old-fashioned look, sprinkle sugar over cookies immediately after removing from oven.

GINGERSNAPS

1-1/4 cups sugar
3/4 cup shortening
1/4 cup molasses
1 egg
2 cups all-purpose
　flour
1-1/2 teaspoons
　baking soda
1/2 teaspoon salt
1 teaspoon cinnamon
1/2 teaspoon ground
　cloves

Combine 1 cup sugar, shortening, molasses, and egg. Beat to blend. Add remaining ingredients, except 1/4 cup sugar. Form into small balls and roll each in 1/4 cup sugar.

Bake at 350 degrees - 8-10 minutes.

Add 1/2 teaspoon pepper to give gingersnaps a little "bite."

COCONUT MACAROONS

2 egg whites
2/3 cup condensed
　milk
1/2 teaspoon salt
2-1/2 cups shredded
　coconut
1 teaspoon vanilla
　flavoring
1/4 teaspoon almond
　flavoring

Beat egg whites until stiff and dry.

In a separate mixing bowl, combine milk, salt, coconut, and flavorings. Mix thoroughly. Carefully fold coconut mixture into egg whites. Drop from teaspoon onto ungreased baking sheet.

Bake at 325 degrees - 15 minutes.

SUGAR COOKIES

1 cup sugar
1/2 cup shortening
1/2 cup butter
2 eggs
2-1/2 cups all-purpose flour
1 teaspoon baking soda
1 teaspoon cream of tartar
2 Tablespoons warm water
1/2 cup fresh squeezed orange juice

Cream sugar, shortening, butter, and eggs together. Add flour, soda, and cream of tartar. Mix thoroughly. Stir in water and orange juice. Dough will be moist.

Cover with plastic wrap. Refrigerate at least 12 hours. When ready to bake, roll out to 1/2-inch thickness. Cut with cookie cutter. Place on ungreased cookie sheet.

Bake at 350 degrees - 8-10 minutes.

Sprinkle with mixture of 3 Tablespoons sugar and 1 teaspoon cinnamon.

PECAN PUFFS

1 egg white
1/4 teaspoon salt
1/4 teaspoon baking
   soda
1 cup light brown
   sugar
3 cups pecan halves

Beat egg white until foamy. Add salt and soda. Add brown sugar. Mix thoroughly. Fold in pecans until all pecans are coated. Drop pecans one at a time onto a greased cookie sheet.

Bake at 300 degrees - 25 minutes or until lightly browned.

Puffs will scorch very easily. Monitor carefully while in oven.

ORANGE BALLS

1 (12-ounce) box
   vanilla wafers
   (crushed into fine
   crumbs)
1-1/2 cups powdered
   sugar
3/4 cup grated
   coconut
3/4 cup chopped
   pecans
1/2 cup orange juice
   concentrate
   (thawed)

Combine wafer crumbs, 1 cup powdered sugar, coconut, pecans, and orange juice. Mix well. Form into 1-inch balls. Roll in remaining 1/2 cup powdered sugar. Store overnight in airtight container.

CARAMEL BROWNIES

1 (18.5-ounce) box German chocolate cake mix

1-1/2 cups chopped pecans

1 (5-ounce) can evaporated milk (divided)

3/4 cup butter (melted)

1 (14-ounce) package caramel candy pieces

1-1/4 cups semi-sweet chocolate chips

Mix together dry cake mix, pecans, 1/2 of evaporated milk, and butter. Divide mixture in half. (It is important to be as accurate as possible when dividing the mix.) Press 1/2 mixture into a generously greased 13x9x2-inch glass baking dish. Mixture will barely cover the bottom. Dampen fingertips and spread over bottom of dish.

Bake at 350 degrees - 8 minutes.

While baking bottom crust, combine remaining milk and caramels in top of double boiler. Stir while candy melts. Pour melted mixture over baked bottom crust. Spread evenly. Sprinkle chocolate chips over top of caramel. Pour remaining batter over layered mixture. Smooth top.

Bake at 350 degrees - 15 minutes.

Brownies must be thoroughly cooled before cutting.

Do you remember *riding a "mop" or "broom" horse and playing cowboys and Indians?*

CHOCOLATE PECAN PIE BARS

CRUST

2 cups all-purpose
flour
1/2 teaspoon salt
1/2 cup butter
(softened)
1/4 cup granulated
sugar
1 (3-ounce) package
cream cheese
(softened)

Sift flour and salt together. Cream butter, sugar, and cream cheese in a separate mixing bowl. Combine with flour. Mix with electric mixer to make a coarse crumbly texture. Press mixture into a greased 13x9x2-inch baking pan.

Bake at 350 degrees 15 minutes or until lightly browned around edges.

FILLING

3 eggs
1 cup granulated sugar
1 cup light corn syrup
2 Tablespoons melted
butter
1 teaspoon vanilla
extract
2 cups chopped
pecans

Combine all ingredients. Mix thoroughly. Pour over baked crust. (Let crust cool 10 minutes before pouring filling.)

TOPPING

2/3 cup milk chocolate
morsels
1 teaspoon shortening

Heat chocolate and shortening over low heat, stirring constantly, until chocolate is melted. Pecan bars should cool thoroughly. Drizzle topping over bars.

HONEY BARS

1 cup sugar
3/4 cup vegetable oil
1 egg
1/4 cup honey
1 teaspoon vanilla
    extract
1-3/4 cups all-purpose
    flour
1 teaspoon baking
    soda
1/4 teaspoon salt
1 teaspoon cinnamon
1 teaspoon nutmeg

Combine sugar, oil, egg, hor
and extract. Beat with elect
mixer until creamy. Sift all d
ingredients. Add to creame
mixture. Mix thoroughly. Spoor
mixture into 15x10x1-inch pan.
Mixture will be very sticky. To
smooth out top of mixture before
baking, sprinkle 1 Tablespoo
flour over top or dampen finge
and lightly press top of bars.

**Bake at 350 degrees 20 minutes or
until lightly browned.**

*For variety, add I cup chopped pecans
to honey bars.*

GLAZE
1 cup powdered sugar
1 teaspoon lemon
    extract

Combine ingredients. Beat to
blend. Pour over warm honey
bars.

*Do you remember the taste of a cold
glass of lemonade after a morning of
working in the garden?*

FROSTED FINGERS

1 (16-ounce) box
   graham crackers
   (divided)
1 cup light brown sugar
   (firmly packed)
1 cup shredded
   coconut
1/2 cup milk
1 stick butter

Line bottom of 13x9x2-inch pan or plastic container with whole graham crackers. Arrange crackers lengthwise. Crush enough crackers to make 1 cup of crumbs to be used in filling.

Combine sugar, coconut, cracker crumbs, milk, and butter in a small saucepan. Heat only long enough to melt butter. Remove from heat and spread over graham crackers. Top filling with a second layer of graham crackers. Crackers must be placed so that perforations on top and bottom layers will match. (These perforated lines will be used as a cutting guide to make neat attractive squares.)

ICING
1-1/2 cups powdered
   sugar
1-2 Tablespoons water

Combine powdered sugar and water. Mix well. Frost squares. Cut along perforations when squares have cooled thoroughly.

STRAWBERRY CHEESECAKE BARS

1-1/4 cups all-purpose
   flour
1/2 cup brown sugar
   (firmly packed)
1/2 cup ground pecans
1/2 cup shortening

Combine all ingredients. Mix until a fine crumbly texture forms (reserve 1/2 cup for topping). Press mixture into a 13x9x2-inch baking pan.

Bake at 350 degrees - 15 minutes or until lightly browned around edges.

FILLING

2 (8-ounce) packages
   cream cheese
   (softened)
3/4 cup granulated
   sugar
2 eggs
1/2 teaspoon rum
   extract
1/2 teaspoon vanilla
   extract

Combine cream cheese, sugar, eggs, and extracts. Beat to blend thoroughly. Pour mixture over hot crust.

Bake at 325 degrees 15-20 minutes or until filling is firm to touch.

TOPPING

1 cup strawberry jam
2 teaspoons lemon
   juice

Combine strawberry jam and lemon juice. Beat until jam is smooth. Spread over cream cheese filling while still warm. Sprinkle with reserve crumb mixture.

Toasted shredded coconut may be combined with topping mixture.

251

AUNT SIS' CONGO BARS

1 pound brown sugar
2/3 cup butter (melted)
3 eggs (beaten)
2-3/4 cups sifted
  all-purpose flour
2-1/2 teaspoons baking
  powder
1/2 teaspoon salt
1 (8-ounce) package
  chocolate chips
1 cup chopped pecans

Cream sugar and butter with electric mixer until smooth and creamy. Add eggs, flour, baking powder, and salt. Beat to blend. Stir in chocolate chips and pecans. Spread into a well-greased 13x9x2-inch greased pan.

Bake at 350 degrees - 35 minutes.

QUICK DESSERT BARS

1 (18.25) box yellow
  cake mix
1 cup brown sugar
1/2 cup butter
2 eggs (beaten)
2 teaspoons vanilla
1 (6-ounce) package
  chocolate chips
1 (6-ounce) package
  butterscotch chips
1 cup chopped pecans

Combine cake mix, sugar, butter, eggs, and vanilla. Mix well. (Batter will be very stiff.) Pour into a greased 13x9x2-inch pan.

Sprinkle chips and pecans over batter. Press slightly with fork.

Bake at 350 degrees - 30 minutes.

Chill thoroughly before cutting into bars. These bars will be very chewy.

CREAMY VANILLA FUDGE

2 cups granulated
  sugar
1/2 cup butter
3/4 cup evaporated
  milk
25 large marshmallows
1 teaspoon vanilla
  extract
8 ounces vanilla chips
1-3/4 cups chopped
  pecans

Combine sugar, butter, and milk in a heavy saucepan. Bring mixture to a boil, stirring constantly. Cook until mixture reaches soft-ball stage. (To test, drop a small amount of mixture from teaspoon into a cup of cool water. Mixture will hold together in a firm ball.) Remove from heat. Add marshmallows, extract, vanilla chips, and pecans to mixture. Stir until marshmallows are dissolved. Drop from a teaspoon onto wax paper.

Should candy not hold its shape when dropped from teaspoon, set pot of candy in pan of ice water and stir vigorously to make firmer.

QUICK FUDGE

3 cups semi-sweet
  chocolate chips
1 (14.5-ounce) can
  condensed milk
1/8 teaspoon salt
1 cup finely chopped
  pecans
2 teaspoons vanilla

Heat chocolate, condensed milk, and salt in a heavy saucepan until chips are melted. Remove from heat. Fold in pecans and vanilla. Turn candy into a 9-inch pan lined with wax paper. Chill until firm (2-3 hours). Cut into squares. Keep in refrigerator.

CREAMY PECAN PRALINES

(pronounced praw-leens or pra-leens)

2 cups sugar

1/4 cup light corn syrup

1/2 cup evaporated milk

4 Tablespoons butter

1/4 teaspoon baking soda

1-1/2 cups chopped pecans (toasted)

Combine all ingredients, except pecans, in a 3-quart aluminum pot. Cook over medium-high heat, stirring constantly, while mixture is cooking. Once mixture has reached a rolling boil, cook until candy reaches softball stage (234 degrees on candy thermometer - approximately 5 minutes). Pour hot mixture into a large mixing bowl. Fold in pecans. Stir with wooden spoon as candy cools. This step may take several minutes. When candy begins to become firm on sides of bowl, drop from a teaspoon onto wax paper.

PECAN PRALINES

3/4 cup unsalted butter

1 cup granulated sugar

1 cup light brown sugar (firmly packed)

1 cup milk

1/2 cup heavy cream

1 Tablespoon vanilla

2-1/2 cups chopped pecans

Melt butter and stir in sugars, milk, and cream. Bring mixture to a boil. Cook on medium-high heat 2 minutes, stirring constantly. Stir in vanilla and pecans. Continue cooking until mixture reaches softball stage (234 degrees on candy thermometer). Remove from heat and continue to beat until candy cools slightly. Beat until candy can be dropped from a teaspoon onto wax paper.

MARTHA WASHINGTON BALLS

2 (16-ounce) boxes
   powdered sugar
1/4 cup butter (melted)
1 (14.5-ounce) can
   condensed milk
1 teaspoon vanilla
   flavoring
4 cups chopped
   pecans
1/2 pound chocolate
   squares
1 small square paraffin

Combine powdered sugar, butter, condensed milk, vanilla, and pecans. Mix thoroughly. Form into 1-inch balls. Place on wax paper. Store in refrigerator for several hours or overnight.

In a small saucepan, melt chocolate and paraffin. Dip balls into hot mixture to coat candy. Place on wax paper until coating is firm (approximately 30-40 minutes).

Do you remember telling ghost stories in the flickering shadows cast by the glow from a kerosene lamp?

A special thanks to Thelma Willis for thirteen years of taking great care to provide excellent service to our customers.

Index

STOKE GABRIEL ENTERPRISES, INC.
P.O. BOX 12060 • ALEXANDRIA, LA 71315

ease send____ copies **Old Black Pot Recipes** ....$12.95 ea. $_____

ease send____ copies **Big Mama's Back In The Kitchen**.Will be available Nov. 1, 2000.$14.95 ea. $_____

ıs postage and handling ....$2.00 ea. $_____

uisiana Residents add sales tax..$ .52 ea. $_____

closed is check ❑   money order ❑ .... Total $_____

ıke checks payable to **Stoke Gabriel Enterprises. - No C.O.D.s**

PLEASE PRINT OR TYPE

ıME_____

)DRESS_____

TY_____ STATE_____ ZIP_____

ALLOW 2 WEEKS FOR DELIVERY

STOKE GABRIEL ENTERPRISES, INC.
P.O. BOX 12060 • ALEXANDRIA, LA 71315

ease send____ copies **Old Black Pot Recipes** ....$12.95 ea. $_____

ease send____ copies **Big Mama's Back In The Kitchen**.Will be available Nov. 1, 2000.$14.95 ea. $_____

ıs postage and handling ....$2.00 ea. $_____

uisiana Residents add sales tax..$ .52 ea. $_____

closed is check ❑   money order ❑ .... Total $_____

ıke checks payable to **Stoke Gabriel Enterprises. - No C.O.D.s**

PLEASE PRINT OR TYPE

ıME_____

)DRESS_____

TY_____ STATE_____ ZIP_____

ALLOW 2 WEEKS FOR DELIVERY

STOKE GABRIEL ENTERPRISES, INC.
P.O. BOX 12060 • ALEXANDRIA, LA 71315

ease send____ copies **Old Black Pot Recipes** ....$12.95 ea. $_____

ease send____ copies **Big Mama's Back In The Kitchen**.Will be available Nov. 1, 2000.$14.95 ea. $_____

ıs postage and handling ....$2.00 ea. $_____

uisiana Residents add sales tax..$ .52 ea. $_____

closed is check ❑   money order ❑ .... Total $_____

ıke checks payable to **Stoke Gabriel Enterprises. - No C.O.D.s**

PLEASE PRINT OR TYPE

ıME_____

)DRESS_____

TY_____ STATE_____ ZIP_____

ALLOW 2 WEEKS FOR DELIVERY

STOKE GABRIEL ENTERPRISES, INC.
P.O. BOX 12060 • ALEXANDRIA, LA 71315

Please send____ copies **Old Black Pot Recipes** ....$12.95 ea. $_____
Please send____ copies **Big Mama's Back In The Kitchen**.........................$14.95 ea. $_____
Plus postage and handling ....$2.00 ea. $_____
Louisiana Residents add sales tax..$ .52 ea. $_____
Enclosed is check ❑   money order ❑ .... Total $_____
Make checks payable to **Stoke Gabriel Enterprises. - No C.O.D.s**

PLEASE PRINT OR TYPE

NAME_____

ADDRESS_____

CITY_____ STATE_____ ZIP_____

ALLOW 2 WEEKS FOR DELIVERY

STOKE GABRIEL ENTERPRISES, INC.
P.O. BOX 12060 • ALEXANDRIA, LA 71315

Please send____ copies **Old Black Pot Recipes** ....$12.95 ea. $_____
Please send____ copies **Big Mama's Back In The Kitchen**.........................$14.95 ea. $_____
Plus postage and handling ....$2.00 ea. $_____
Louisiana Residents add sales tax..$ .52 ea. $_____
Enclosed is check ❑   money order ❑ .... Total $_____
Make checks payable to **Stoke Gabriel Enterprises. - No C.O.D.s**

PLEASE PRINT OR TYPE

NAME_____

ADDRESS_____

CITY_____ STATE_____ ZIP_____

ALLOW 2 WEEKS FOR DELIVERY

STOKE GABRIEL ENTERPRISES, INC.
P.O. BOX 12060 • ALEXANDRIA, LA 71315

Please send____ copies **Old Black Pot Recipes** ....$12.95 ea. $_____
Please send____ copies **Big Mama's Back In The Kitchen**.........................$14.95 ea. $_____
Plus postage and handling ....$2.00 ea. $_____
Louisiana Residents add sales tax..$ .52 ea. $_____
Enclosed is check ❑   money order ❑ .... Total $_____
Make checks payable to **Stoke Gabriel Enterprises. - No C.O.D.s**

PLEASE PRINT OR TYPE

NAME_____

ADDRESS_____

CITY_____ STATE_____ ZIP_____

ALLOW 2 WEEKS FOR DELIVERY